PROTOCOL OF THE THIRTY-FIFTH COLLOQUY: 25 FEBRUARY 1979

THE ROLE OF THE CHRISTIAN BISHOP IN ANCIENT SOCIETY

HENRY CHADWICK
DEAN OF CHRIST CHURCH, OXFORD UNIVERSITY, ENGLAND

EDWARD C. HOBBS & WILHELM WUELLNER, *Editors*

WIPF & STOCK · Eugene, Oregon

Wipf and Stock Publishers
199 W 8th Ave, Suite 3
Eugene, OR 97401

The Role of the Christian Bishop in Ancient Society
Protocol of the Thirty-fifth Colloquy, 25 February 1979
By Chadwick, Henry

ISBN 13: 978-1-62032-027-3
Publication date 3/1/2012
Previously published by Center for Hermeneutical Studies in Hellenistic and Modern Culture, 1980

TABLE OF CONTENTS

THE ROLE OF THE CHRISTIAN BISHOP IN ANCIENT SOCIETY

HENRY CHADWICK

1. The Bishop's Authority Within the Church.

The early Christian bishop emerges as the leader of the local Christian community based upon the town. The first missionaries had concentrated upon the urban population, and almost all the evidence concerning the shape of second-century Christianity shows the churches to be organised round the towns. Ancient towns were, for the most part, small by our standards. Rome, Antioch, Alexandria, and Constantinople were large enough for an individual to be lost in the crowd; but most "cities" of antiquity are quite small communities in market towns, provided with a defensive wall in case of trouble. It was therefore possible for the bishop to know, and to be known personally by, his flock. To his people he has the authority of a shepherd, called to model himself upon the example of Christ the Chief Shepherd (1 Peter 5, 2-4). His authority is acknowledged in the consent of the plebs to his consecration.[1] But the plebs, as experience showed, was vulnerable to faction, and soon an increasingly important role in the selection of a bishop was played by the bishops of neighbouring churches who came to lay hands upon the candidate at his consecration, and who represented not only their own churches but also the universal Church. No small part of the aura attaching to the local bishop depended upon this catholicity of recognition. In synod he represented his people. To his people he represented the "synod;" that is, he was a sign of unity and universality among the federation of local churches bonded together in eucharistic communion, spread through the Mediterranean world of the Roman empire. Accordingly, while each local church felt itself to be a self-sufficient fellowship in which all the essential elements of the universal church are present, yet the independence and autonomy of this local community is limited by the mutual care that local churches must have for each other. When at the end of the first century the church at Corinth decided to sack its clergy and to install a new lot, their brothers in Rome were much distressed and, apologising not for intervening but for not having interfered more quickly, wrote to admonish the Corinthians for having supposed the authority of their pastors to rest exclusively upon their consent. Rather must they understand that the shepherds of the flock derive their tenure from the succession from the apostles themselves and from the inherent nature of their sacramental functions as ministers of the word and sacrament. The Roman church accordingly invites the Corinthian church to reinstate the dispossessed clergy and so to submit "not to our will but to God's," knowing that if they refuse they must answer for it at the Last Judgement. The Corinthian Christians have failed to realise that the ordering of the community of the new covenant is no less precise, and no less divinely given, than the hierarchical priesthood of the Old Testament with its clearcut distinctions of function between priest and layman. The New Testament principle of obedience to the pastors who must give account for the souls of their flock (Heb. 13, 17; 1 Thess. 5, 12f.) is already being given a powerful reinforcement from Old Testament typology.

---

[1]The consent of the plebs: see Hippolytus, *Apostolic Tradition* 2: "let the bishop be ordained who is elected by all the people. ... With the agreement of all let the bishops lay hands on him and the presbyters stand by in silence." For the late fourth century see Basil, *Ep.* 230, telling the magistrates of Nicopolis, who evidently thought otherwise, that the appointment of bishops is in the hands of the clergy though their choice requires ratification by the laity; now the bishops have selected their man, it is for the magistrates to support them.

The schism in the community at Corinth was particularly embarrassing because it became generally discussed in the town: dirty linen was being washed in public, and pagan insult added to Christian injury (1 Clement 47). The existence of competing groups caused problems for visitors who could find that they had caused great offence by accepting hospitality from the wrong body of clergy (hence 1 Clement's emphasis on the virtue of hospitality exemplified by Abraham, Lot, and Rahab the harlot, "saved by faith and hospitality"). In short, the internal organisation of the Christian community at Corinth was not, and could not be, a purely private domestic matter; it affected other people elsewhere, and had immediate impact upon the standing of the church in the "secular" community. Clement of Rome tells them that the local church is to be the earthly counterpart of the heavenly: let the Corinthians imitate the angelic chorus which, though numbering ten thousand times ten thousand (and therefore liable to find it hard to keep together), nevertheless chant in unison and on the beat: "Holy, holy, holy ...".

This concept of a correspondence between the church in heaven and the church on earth goes back to the very roots of the earliest eucharistic theology. It provides Ignatius of Antioch with his principal argument for concentrating the local church in communion with the bishop, who is, according to Ignatius, the counterpart (*typos*) of God. Hence his monarchical presidency. The early Christian communities had deep feelings against having two bishops in one city.[2] Parallel jurisdictions in the same geographical area were very uncongenial. The eighth canon of the Council of Nicaea, 325, legislates for the full recognition of the orders of Novatianist clergy on the reconciliation of their flocks to the *ecclesia catholica* (subject to their willingness to accept to communion digamists[3] and those who have served their penitential term after lapse in time of persecution), except that the Novatianist bishop is to rank as a presbyter under the authority of the sitting catholic incumbent, even if he may retain the episcopal title with the consent of the catholic bishop. Alternatively he may become a "country bishop" or *chorepiskopos*; that is, a bishop with wholly rural responsibility which was in process of being subordinated to the city bishop. (A decade before Nicaea a council at Ancyra [Ankara] had restricted the powers of country bishops in ordinations. A council at Neocaesarea shortly afterwards explained that while city bishops are successors of the twelve apostles, country bishops are successors of the seventy sent out by the Lord according to Luke 10; they may concelebrate the liturgy in recognition of their ministry to the poor. A council of Antioch four or five years after Nicaea insists on their subordination to the city bishop of their region. Basil's *Epp.* 53-54 illustrate the problem: the city bishops did not trust the country bishops to be strict against simony and against nepotism.)[4] The Nicene canon about the Novatianists exemplifies a conviction that the church has "one God, one Christ, one bishop," a Roman slogan of the time of the Novatianist schism in Rome in 251 (Eusebius, *H.E.* VI 43, 11; Cyprian, *Ep.* 49,2) which was shouted as an acclamation by the crowd in the Circus Maximus in 358 when Constantius agreed to allow Pope Liberius to return from exile (Theodoret, *H.E.* II 17, 6).

If to us it may seem a little extravagant to hold that it inheres in the logic of monotheism that in one city, there may be only one bishop, to the ancients the argument would have had a familiar ring. At the end of the third century an imperial

---

[2]Evidence for the principle of not having two bishops in one city is collected in Joseph Bingham's *Antiquities of the Christian Church* II, 13 (1708 and later editions).

[3]Novatianists were not agreed among themselves about the admission of digamists to communion, the Phrygians being rigorist: Socrates, *H.E.* V 22, 60. All agreed that digamy was a bar to ordination.

[4]*Chorepiscopi*: a good survey by H. Leclercq in *Dict. d'arch. et de liturgie chr.* III/1, art. "Chorévêques."

panegyrist buttressed the authority of Diocletian and the tetrarchy with the reflection that, with four winds, four elements, etc., fourness corresponds to the essential nature of things. A few years later Eusebius of Caesarea suggested that Constantine's elimination of successively superfluous colleagues until he was sole emperor was a providential arrangement to provide an earthly counterpart for the divine Monarch. No doubt there were also less mystical reasons for thinking it right to establish a monarchical episcopate. The conflict with heresy made it a practical necessity to make one presiding figure the personal focus of ecclesial unity in the local congregation. The second century conflicts with gnostic heresy, with the consequent movement towards greater standardisation and uniformity of expression, surely strengthened rather than weakened the authority of the bishop in relation to his flock. At the same time, however, the pressure of other churches on a dissenting community, or other bishops on a dissenting colleague, tended to diminish the autonomy of a local church and its bishop. Cyprian might indeed declare boldly that every bishop is equal, as every apostle was, and is answerable to God alone. But one hardly needs to read between the lines of his writings to see that in his opinion the episcopate ought to be unanimous, that decisions in synod are not reached by majority votes that preserve the conscientious dissent of the minority, and that the individual bishop has a duty to discern and bring himself into line with this unanimity. *Episcopatus unus est, cuius a singulis in solidum pars tenetur* sounds like a trained lawyer's way of affirming a truth dear to Cyprian's heart, that each local church possesses all the essential elements of the universal Church. But it does not mean for Cyprian that every bishop is allowed to be "a law unto himself," or that the principal function of the Holy Spirit in the fellowship of the Christian society is to foster mutual tolerance amid the continual dissension.

The diminution of the autonomy of the local bishop was increased still further early in the fourth century by the Nicene canons which created the authority of the metropolitan of the civil province. The fourth Nicene canon gives the bishop of the civil metropolis a power of veto over episcopal elections (it does not yet go so far as to make him always the principal consecrator). St. Matthew's gospel (18, 20) preserves a saying of the Lord, "Where two or three are gathered in my name, there am I in the midst of them," which was interpreted as defining the quorum for a valid episcopal election. In case of any controversy or division it was prudent to have three bishops as one's consecrators, as Novatian did at Rome (Cornelius in Eusebius, *H.E.* VI 43, 8). In the same decade Cyprian claims that in North Africa and "in almost all provinces" the custom was for a new bishop to be chosen from among members of the local congregation and ordained by neighbouring bishops of the same province (*Ep.* 67, 5). In 314 the Council of Arles protested against consecrations carried out by only one bishop, and desired seven, while allowing three as the minimum (canon 20). At Nicaea the attendance of all bishops of the province was recognised as the ideal; but it is granted that a quorum of three may act, subject to the written consent of their absent colleagues and the metropolitan's veto (canon 4). However, the Arian author of the *Apostolic Constitutions*, and of the *Apostolic Canons* appended thereto, was reflecting an older usage when he allows the validity of consecrations by "two or three" bishops (*AC* iii.20; viii.27 and 47, 1 = *Ap.Can.* 1); he is writing in Syria, perhaps at Antioch, about 360, mainly revising older material. (The set of Apostolic Canons looks like the Constitutor's personal creation.)[5] Episcopal consecrations by only two bishops were almost always partisan. Their validity was sure to be questioned by the opposing faction and upheld by faithful supporters. In Spain, where the metropolitical structure was slow to develop, Priscillian could be ordained at Avila by only two bishops in 381, with the consent of the plebs.[6] When in 457 the news of

[5]On the Apostolic Canons see F.X. Funk, *Die apostolische Konstitutionen* (1891); E. Schwartz, *Gesammelte Schriften* 5 (1963) 2-4-45; above all, C.H. Turner in *JTS* 16 (1915) 523-538.

[6]Priscillian's consecration: see H. Chadwick, *Priscillian of Avila* (1976) 33.

the emperor Marcian's death reached Alexandria, the mob, hostile to their Chalcedonian bishop Proterius, rushed to the Caesareum to have Timothy the Cat installed as their true (monophysite) bishop, but could find only one bishop ready to lay hands upon him. The hermit bishop Peter the Iberian had to be dragged from his sickbed to make a second; and later anti-Chalcedonian writers claimed that he was actually the third, thereby complying with the Nicene minimum, and eliminating a source of grave embarrassment in controversy. That Timothy had the consent of the plebs was certain: his elevation led to the murder of poor Proterius.[7]

Accordingly, there was much good sense in the Nicene provision for control by the metropolitan. The metropolitical structure in turn came to be felt to be inadequate, and to need guidance from above by the creation of patriarchates. At Nicaea a desire on the part of Libya to be independent of Alexandrian control was crushed by the sixth canon, which lays down that the supra-provincial authority of Alexandria is justified by analogy with that exercised also by Rome and Antioch.[8] The patriarchate of Antioch was reduced by the achievement of Juvenal of Jerusalem in the mid-fifth century, who created a patriarchate for the mother see of Christendom at the expense of the jurisdiction of Antioch.[9] Antioch also lost control of Cyprus, where the church asserted itself to be autocephalous. The great see of New Rome at Constantinople was in time to become the dominant patriarchate in the Greek East, eventually "the ecumenical patriarchate" (the title, later to cause much offence to Pope Gregory the Great, was in use from the middle of the fifth century).[10] The patriarchs of Constantinople had grave initial difficulties in establishing their authority, partly because of a desire by metropolitans in Asia Minor to retain their independence, partly because of political rivalry between Alexandria and the upstart capital on the Bosphorus. The imperial government in the fourth century liked dividing provinces, but simultaneously grouping them under larger units called "dioceses." At the time of the Council of Constantinople of 381, the second "ecumenical council," some were inclined to expect the bishop at the administrative centre of the civil "diocese" to exercise leadership and some appellate jurisdiction over provincial metropolitans. In practice, the older order continued to assert itself. To the distress of the bishops of Alexandria the see of Constantinople slowly came to exercise considerable authority not only in Thrace but also in Asia Minor. But no patriarch of Constantinople ever exercised the power enjoyed in Egypt by the see of Alexandria, whose bishop had the traditional right to consecrate every bishop under his jurisdiction. The imperial court sought to sweeten Theophilus of Alexandria by inviting him to be the principal consecrator when John Chrysostom was brought from Antioch to Constantinople in 398. But Theophilus soon had reason to resent John's very active exercise of jurisdiction, e.g. in the investigation of the consecration fee that bishops in the province of Asia had been paying to the metropolitan of Ephesus, a scandal which John dealt with in a most unbending

---

[7]Timothy Aelurus' consecration is grippingly narrated in the *Life of Peter the Iberian* (ed. and trans. Raabe, 1895) where Peter is the second bishop specially brought in, not the third as in Zacharias Scholasticus IV 1. Severus of Antioch (*Select Letters* ed. Brooks, ii 3, transl. I 224-5) rejects as a lie the story that Timothy was ordained by only two rather than by three bishops. Pope Pelagius I, 556-61, whose election was highly controversial, could only find two bishops to consecrate him, and the third was in presbyteral orders: *Liber Pontificalis* I 303 Duchesne.

[8]On the sixth canon of Nicaea there is a justly famous paper by Schwartz in the *Berlin Academy Sitzungsberichte*, 1930. I have tried to take the story further in *Harvard Theological Review* 53 (1960) 171-195.

[9]On Juvenal of Jerusalem see Honigmann in *Dumbarton Oaks Papers* V.

[10]On the rise of the patriarchate of Constantinople see now the last section of Gilbert Dagron's admirable book on the origins of the city, *Naissance d'une capitale* (1974).

manner (like a man with no knees, they said of him). In the Nestorius affair, the see of Alexandria triumphed over New Rome apparently decisively. The patriarch of Constantinople was branded as a heretic and eventually exiled to the Egyptian desert. Even so, each successive conflict between Alexandria and Constantinople left the new patriarchate at the capital in a stronger position than before. As long as Cyril presided at Alexandria, Alexandrian influence remained predominant. His successor Dioscorus was a much less political animal than Cyril; a zealot who disliked theological compromise and preferred to stand on principles, Dioscorus of Alexandria took the first and fatal step towards detaching the Egyptian church to become a separated body. He and his suffragans broke with Rome and the West as well as with Constantinople, and thereby shattered the traditional standing of the Alexandrian patriarchate.

One might expect the consequence to be the acquisition by Constantinople of powers in the Greek churches comparable to those exercised in the West by the bishops of old Rome. That it was not so is evidence of the deep strength of feeling in the Greek churches that authority grows "from the bottom upwards," and that the eucharistic communion of the local churches is the foundation of all communion. In the West, on the other hand, communion with the see where St. Peter and St. Paul taught and died a glorious death was instinctively felt to be the criterion and touchstone of authentic ecclesiality. Even the churches in North Africa, which held the most Cyprianic views on the equality of all bishops as brothers in the Lord and reacted with vehemence against any suggestion that there could be an *episcopus episcoporum*, nevertheless assented without reservation to the concept of the see of Peter and Paul as the focus of unity and universality.

Without the internal structure of authority within the Church there could have been no wider role for bishops to play in "secular" society. The bishop's power-base, so to speak, lay always in the allegiance of his flock to the ministry of word and sacrament and pastoral care of which he is the focus. To the faithful he represented not merely a properly constituted officer of the community but an instrument of divine grace, inasmuch as his ordination is a sacramental act conferring a charismatic gift of grace appropriate to the office (1 Tim. 4, 14; 2 Tim. 1, 6).

2. The Bishop's Social Role Within the Church.

The bishop's responsibility for hospitality has already been alluded to above. In the first instance, it was a responsibility for travelling missionaries; then for *peregrini* generally (Ambrose, *de officiis* ii 103). His share (normally a quarter of the offerings of the faithful) of the church treasury was also the resource on which he called for supporting the poor, the protection of whom was one of his prime responsibilities. In the fifties of the third century the community in Rome had on its payroll one bishop, 46 presbyters, 7 deacons, 7 sub-deacons, 42 acolytes, 52 exorcists, readers, and door-keepers, and more than 1500 widows and distressed persons, "all of whom were fed by the grace and kindness of the Lord" (Cornelius in Eusebius, *H.E.* VI 43, 11). The distribution of alms to the poor was a plentiful source of discontent among the recipients. Augustine confesses that he finds the problems of the administration of church finance altogether hateful (*Ep.* 126, 9), so numerous are the resentments created over money matters. On the anniversary of the bishop's ordination, his *natalis* or birthday, he was expected to give a general dinner for the poor on the church roll (Augustine, *S Frangip.* 2 p. 189). The bishop would also be entrusted with young children made wards of the Church (Augustine, *Epp.* 252-255), a responsibility not very easy for the clergy to discharge when their wards turned out to be turbulent teenage girls (see a classic papyrus document from Egypt on this subject in Mitteis-Wilcken, *Chrestomathie*). Orphans would be taken into the bishop's household (Augustine,

S 176, 2). This special care for the poor, for waifs and strays, is often mentioned in epitaphs of bishops besides the excellence of their instruction--"teaching apostolic doctrine so as to make all his congregation weep for their sins" (*ILCV* 967; cf. 989 on generosity to the poor). The church's financial needs naturally imposed on the bishop and his staff a care for church property, after the advent of Constantine made it legally possible for bequests to be made. The church's property interests sometimes needed to be defended in the courts (Augustine, ep. 21, 5); Augustine, *Ep.* 99, records an uncomfortable dispute about the property of his church at Hippo. By A.D. 400 it was common practice for the more devout in Syria and Asia Minor to bequeath to the church a third of their estate (Basil the Great, *Or.* 7, *PG* 31, 299; Greg. Nyss. *de pauperum amore*, *PG* 46, 466B; Chrysostom, *de eleemos. et hospit. hom.* 23 *PG* 63, 725; *in Matt.* 88 *PG* 57, 779). In the West the expected benefaction was the share that an additional child would have received (Jerome, *Ep.* 120, 1; Augustine, *en. ps.* 38, 12; S 86, 11-14, and esp. 355 rejecting as wrong the bequeathing of all one's property to the church in disregard of any family claimants).

The apostle Paul told the Corinthians that they must not take their grievances against one another to the lawcourts but settle disagreements by asking members of the congregation to arbitrate. Arbitrations became a major preoccupation of bishops.[11] In third-century Syria it was the rule for the bishop to set each Monday to hear cases, and to be assisted by his presbyters and deacons; the court sat on Mondays to give time for negotiation towards reconciliation in time for the eucharist on the following Sunday (*Didascalia* ii, 47 p. 111 Connolly = *Apost. Const.* ii, 47, partly taken over by *Statuta Ecclesiae Antiqua* 14). Constantine even allowed a civil case to be transferred, at the request of either party, to the bishop's court and enacted that in that event there should be no appeal from the bishop's decision (*C.Th.* i, 27, 1). It is important that the earliest evidence for the operation of the episcopal court or *audientia* shows an overriding concern for the amicable reconciliation of the parties, and that "justice" is a secondary matter. A striking illustration of the same point may be found in Gregory of Nyssa's *Life* of the third-century missionary in Pontus, Gregory Thaumaturgus (*PG* 46, 925). Augustine found that his duties as arbitrator and judge were in general distasteful, certainly a major distraction from his spiritual duties. In his experience those who brought cases before the bishop were not the good faithful members of his congregation, but persons with a consistent record for being tiresome and contentious (*en. ps.* 118 S 24). Moreover, it brought the bishop into some *odium* if, as was often the case, the contention was between rich and poor: to decide in favour of the rich man was to invite accusations of upholding a class interest and toadying the powerful, and to decide in favour of the poor man was to invite accusations of bribery (*en. ps.* 25, 13; Ambrose *off.* ii,125).

Constantine was asked by an incredulous high official whether he really meant to make the bishop's decision final, and replied that he did, that it was the secular judge's duty to see that the bishop's decision was strictly enforced, and that, because of the freedom from restriction in the admissibility of evidence that distinguished a bishop's court from a secular court, and because of the charismatic powers of the bishops

---

[11]On the bishop's court, *audientia episcopalis*, see J.M. Bakhuizen van den Brink in *Mededelingen d. Akad. Wet. Amsterdam* 19 (1956) 145-301. On Byzantine Egypt, H.I. Bell in *Byzantion* 1 (1924) 139; Steinwenter, *BZ* 30 (1929) 660; his article in *Reallexikon für Antike und Christentum* I, s.v. *Audientia episcopalis*, is a disappointment. On transfer to the bishop from civil process, see, e.g. Ambrose, *Ep.* 82 (an arbitration); for a criminal case, Basil *Ep.* 286 asking the civil authority to leave to him the discipline of some thieves caught stealing clothes at a large church festival. Synesius, *Ep.* 105 mentions *scholastikoi* of the Alexandrian church. The intimate cooperation between bishops and magistrates in keeping down the poor is bitterly attacked by Jerome, *in Mich.* I 2, 9-10, p. 457 Vallarsi, as fatal to the bishop's plausibility in his prime duty to act as protector of the poor against the powerful.

as holy men capable of discerning the hearts of men, a bishop was not in need of correction by a higher court (*Const. Sirm.* 1 of 333). A similar doctrine of episcopal charism is found in an astonishing document of a Roman synod of 378 which undertook to defend Pope Damasus from the embarrassing charge of responsibility for homicide at the time of his election in 366, when an ugly riot cost the lives of 137 of the plebs who were divided between two candidates.[12] The synod claimed that thanks to this charismatic power of discernment, bishops had no need, as secular judges, to resort to judicial torture to ascertain the truth in cases of conflicting testimony (*PL* 13, 578). That very holy men could discern guilt and innocence was recognised by pagan and Christian alike in late antiquity (e.g. Porphyry's *Life of Plotinus* 11; *Life of Pythagoras* 13, 54; Rufinus, *Historia Monachorum* 16). Augustine, no doubt realistically, declines to claim any special powers of discernment for his decisions. He also remarks (*City of God* 19, 6) that the deplorable use of torture by secular judges leads many innocent men to confess to crimes they have not committed, and censures the use of torture as "abhorrent to Christians" (*Ep.* 104, 16). Whether the same abhorrence was felt by Pope Leo the Great in his inquisition into the crypto-Manichees discovered to be numerous among his congregation in 443 (an inquisition in which the bishop of Rome was assisted not only by other bishops and inferior clergy but also by eminent lay assessors) is unhappily uncertain (Leo *Ep.* 15, 16); he seems to have been content if the secular arm applied methods stronger than that gentle persuasion which alone was appropriate for the clergy. But a Manichee process was exceptional. The severest punishment of a bishop's court was, at worst, likely to be corporal punishment; and even that was widely held to be ruled out. The sixth-century bishop of the island of Samos who found that he needed a private prison to restrain delinquent clergy (Moschus, *Pratum* 108) may have been unique. (Imperial legislation was against private prisons.) The Arian author of the Apostolic Constitutions directs, in the 27th Apostolic Canon, that clergy may not beat sinners. The Canonists Zonaras and Balsamon oppose the view that they might hand the chastisement over to laymen; Balsamon allowing a possible exception for schoolmasters in holy orders, but insisting that even they may never cane "in anger and fury" (Rhalli-Potli II 680).

Accusations against the bishop himself could raise complex issues, since internal ecclesiastical faction could give unhappy motives for prosecution against which the bishop needed proper protection. The council of Constantinople of 382 (in the canon 6 ascribed mistakenly to the council of 381) lays down that a charge on a purely secular matter may be brought against a bishop by anyone under normal procedure; but on any ecclesiastical charge no accusation might be brought by a heretic, a schismatic, an excommunicate person, or anyone himself uncleared of an accusation. Subject to the exclusion of these categories, a charge against a bishop must come first to the provincial synod, from which appeal could be made to a greater synod constituted by the bishops of the civil Diocese whose decision would be final. No appeal could be made to the emperor or to the civil courts or to an ecumenical council as if greater than that of the Diocese under its patriarch. (This canon provided a model for later legislation, e.g. Justinian, *Novel* 183, 21.)

Delicate judicial issues were raised for bishops by the right of asylum, especially when the church's altars were sought by armed bandits on the run.[13] Although the right of asylum was widely criticised (and not, of course, always respected), both Augustine (*S. Guelf.* 25 p. 528) and John Chrysostom (Socrates *H.E.* VI 5) defended it. In the case of pagan shrines the right of asylum was held to depend on a special privilege granted by the emperor. The Christians raised awkward problems by claiming

[12]On the Roman synod of 378 see Chadwick, *Priscillian of Avila* 128-9.

[13]Asylum was important for debtors and runaway slaves. Jerome (*in Esai.* xvi p. 690) picks out high interest rates with the money lenders as the prime cause of sedition in cities, driving many into hopeless debt.

the right of asylum for any altar. Justinian's final compromise was to allow asylum for oppressed persons, but not for criminals (*Nov.* 17, 7 pr. of 535).

The most frequent duty of bishops was to intercede for members of their flock when they were in trouble with the courts or the fisc. Augustine found these intercessory activities time-consuming and irritating, but recognised that the judicial and fiscal system made them necessary (*Ep.* 151, 2 and 152-153). Otherwise the oppressed would never get justice at all.

The patronage role assumed by fourth-century bishops meant or could mean power. Athanasius of Alexandria (*HA* 78, 1) remarks that the bishop's freedom from *munera* and his role as patron gave a motive leading ambitious men to seek holy orders. The Christian emperors were quickly known to be easily accessible to bishops seeking protection for the oppressed. The council of Serdica (343) observed that the name of bishop was being brought into disrepute by bishops going to court to seek favours for their relatives and friends (canons 8 and 13). Moreover, the quasi-judicial role of the bishop's court became a source of revenue to the see,[14] since no doubt to protect themselves against a flood of arbitrations the bishops thought it necessary to charge the standard legal fees. In the 350s Silvanus, bishop of Tarsus, thought it prudent to have a lay adviser to read all the documents submitted by the contestants (Socrates, *H.E.* VII 37, 17). This appears to be the first evidence for the creation of the office of the defensor ecclesiae, a lay lawyer on the bishop's staff who, from early in the fifth century (Pope Zosimus *Ep.* 9, 3), might take holy orders, and would particularly look after the church's legal interests (e.g. Possidius, *V. Aug.* 12 where the defensor ecclesiae appeals to the civil courts after a Circumcellion attack). At the time of the councils of Ephesus (449) and Chalcedon (451) a prominent role is played by the defensor of the church of Alexandria, who is in presbyteral orders (*Act. Chalc.* i, 222, 235, 305, 311, etc.).

It is hardly surprising that episcopal elections were normally a source of unrest and disorder (Socrates *H.E.* VII 40 so comments). The council of Serdica records its outrage at the practice of bribing a claque of laity to shout for a particular candidate (can. 2). It was common for bishops nearing their end to try to avert a riot by nominating their successor, as Augustine himself tried (unsuccessfully) to do. In a surprisingly numerous proportion of cases, the problem of the succession was solved by the dominance of a particular family, round which the church in a town had first been formed and which then expected to supply a suitable candidate. In the second century Polycrates of Ephesus was proud to claim that seven of his relatives had been bishops (Eusebius *H.E.* V 24, 6). In Mesopotamia and especially in Armenia (see *Trull. can.* 33) it was normal for a see to remain in the family, however widely extended the concept of family might be. Elsewhere the practice was criticised as nepotism. In the 460s Pope Hilarus complains that in Spain bishops treat their see not as a divine gift but as hereditary property that they can dispose of by will (*Ep.* 15 p. 162 Thiel). Origen bitterly complains of hereditary bishoprics (*H. Num.* 22, 4). A similarly negative view appears in the 76th Apostolic Canon. On the other hand Prudentius rhapsodises over the family of the Valerii which had produced a succession of bishops for Saragossa (*Perist.* IV 79-80, supported by the record of the early fourth-century council of Elvira, and probably also that of Saragossa 380).[15]

In 335 the bishop of Constantinople was nearing his end and was asked which of his clergy he wished to see as his successor. He replied that he thought the church should choose between two: if a good teacher of the faith was the prime requirement,

---

[14]Justinian found it necessary to put a ceiling on the legal fees and tips charged in church courts: *CJ* i, 4, 29 (530).

[15]Avitus of Vienne succeeded his father Hesychius in the see, and his brother Apollinaris became bishop of Valence: Duchesne, *Fastes* I 184.

they should elect Paul--but if they wanted someone good at public affairs and negotiating with the authorities, then the right man was Macedonius. In the event, Paul was so anxious to be bishop that he got homself ordained by some bishops who happened to be in Constantinople (there was no city in which it was so easy to constitute a quick synod out of casual episcopal visitors); but without the consent of the metropolitan of Heraclea and without the approval of Constantine so that it was easy for his opponents to have him synodically expelled (see Sozomen iii, 3-4). Ascetically minded believers were distressed at the quality of bishops received under the system of popular suffrage. Augustine remarks to Jerome that wealthy candidates with low educational and spiritual qualifications are often preferred to poor men with high qualifications (*Ep.* 167, 18, written, it should be recalled, to a scholarly presbyter who had once much wanted to be bishop of Rome).[16] The standard of education among bishops varied quite widely. Illiterate bishops are a favourite butt for the mockery of the half-educated, observes Augustine (*Cat. rud.* 13). The council of Chalcedon included at least one illiterate bishop (from Lycia; *Act. Chalc.* i, 1070, Latin version). On the other hand, by the fifth century important sees could be held by ex-senators, men like Nectarius of Constantinople (381-97), or Thalassius who was put into the see of Cappadocian Caesarea just as he was to be gazetted for the office of praetorian prefect (Socrates VII 48). In the West the best known of the great aristocrats to become bishops are Ambrose of Milan and Paulinus of Nola. But in the fifth century a bishopric was occasionally an enforced exile, as for Cyrus of Panopolis (Malalas XIV 362), and for two western emperors who suffered deposition, Avitus and Glycerius. Petronius bishop of Bologna is said by Gennadius to have been praetorian prefect (*Vir. inl.* 42). If we are asking what social role was expected of a fifth-century bishop, the answer can be easily seen in Ennodius' *Life* of Epiphanius of Pavia (Ticinum). Epiphanius' authority is grounded in his spirituality as an ascetic and holy man, seen in e.g. his abstinence from baths and his abstinence from an evening meal. At midday he would be hospitable over luncheon. He sought to protect the poor and to make intercession for the oppressed. From Odovacar he won five years' tax exemption for his city. He gathered money to redeem prisoners of war. In the quarrels between the princes, he was trusted by both sides, and was accordingly asked to act as ambassador--for Ricimer to Anthemius, for Nepos to Euric, from Theodoric to Gundobad the Burgundian king.

The redemption of prisoners of war was the one cause for which bishops thought it morally right to sell church plate (Ambrose, *off.* ii.70, 142-3; Possidius *V. Aug.* 24; Justinian's law of 529, *CJ* I 2, 21, allows its sale for no other purpose). The principle was taken to notable lengths by Acacius bishop of Amida (Diyabakir) on the upper Tigris. He sold his church plate to redeem not Roman citizens captured by the Persians, but Persian prisoners whom the Roman soldiers would not release (Socrates VII 21). It was an extension of the principle that Christian charitable aid to the poor should not discriminate in favour of church members but should have no criterion other than need (see an eloquent statement by Atticus of Constantinople in Socrates *H.E.* VII 25).

The neutrality of bishops between factions or between warring nations often led to embassies. In their role as ambassadors, bishops shared with philosophers the aura of authority which brought ambassadorial responsibilities to a number of pagan philosophers of the fourth century (Themistius, Iphicles of Epirus, and others listed by J.G. Matthews in *Reallexikon für Antike und Christentum*, art. "Gesandschaft"). The earliest example is Eusebius bishop of Nicomedia sent by Licinius to negotiate terms with Constantine in 324. Ammianus Marcellinus records a number of instances

---

[16]Jerome's commentary on Ecclesiastes contains some sad observations on the popular preference for unscholarly bishops (ix 11, p. 465; x 5 p. 471). "Whenever you see a much applauded preacher, be sure he is a fool" (ix 17, p. 467).

where Christian clergy acted as intermediaries between the Roman army and barbarians, the most interesting of which is the bishop of Bezabde in Mesopotamia whose city was being besieged by the Persians. The bishop went to the Persian camp for parley. Unhappily for him, the next Persian attack was directed at just the weakest part of the wall, and it was suspected that the bishop's neutrality had passed into treachery (Ammian. XX 7,9; the other instances are XXXI 12, 8-9; 15, 6; XXIX 5, 15). The Christians felt themselves and were felt by others to stand outside the conflicts between Roman and barbarian, and somehow to represent the cause of humanity. On the other hand, some bishops wholly identified themselves with the Roman struggle against the barbarian invasions. Jerome so writes of Exsuperius of Toulouse (*Ep.* 123, 16). According to the *Life of Germanus* bishop of Auxerre, he went to Britain, beset by Pelagianism, with a military force, being himself *dux belli*. He was happily granted the miraculous Alleluia victory in which no bloodshed was necessary.

The more usual Christian view was that the proper role of bishops is to pray for the emperor and his army. Victory in battle is the gift of heaven, and nothing is more likely to make and keep heaven propitious than the devout prayers and holy lives of the people of God. Origen (*c. Cels.* 8, 73) observes that pagan priests are not enlisted in war so that they may offer the customary sacrifices with unsullied hands, and justifies Christian withdrawal from military service on the ground that by their prayers the faithful "destroy all daemons who stir up wars" and "are of more help to the emperors than the soldiers." The ancient Solemn Prayers following the gospel for Good Friday in the Roman Missal probably go back in substance to the fourth century:

> Omnipotens sempiterne deus, in cuius manu sunt omnium temporum potestates et omnia iura regnorum, respice propitius ad Romanum benignus imperium, ut gentes quae in sua feritate confidunt potentiae tuae dextera comprimantur.

The preceding bidding exhorts the faithful to pray that God may "subdue to the emperors all barbarian nations for our perpetual peace."

Wars on earth, explains John Cassian (*Coll.* 8, 13) reflect the internecine wars among the demons.

That the right form of worship is essential if heaven is to be propitious is an axiom of ancient society. The axiom lies at the root of the pagan persecutions of the Christians, as also of the deep unpopularity of the Jews in the Greco-Roman world. The Christians introduced an even greater passion into the matter by their belief that right worship also presupposed right doctrine, and that therefore heresy or schism would, if long tolerated, or regarded as a matter of indifference, provoke the wrath of the Lord. The ferocity of sectarian conflicts in the fourth and later centuries cannot be understood without the centrality of this axiom. In the fifth and sixth centuries the Chalcedonians are sure that the defeats of the imperial armies are the consequence of the prevalence of so many Monophysites; and vice versa. To give illustrations is superfluous, since the assumption is to be met constantly throughout the period in innumerable sources. One vivid example may serve. After the emperor Theodosius I had defeated Magnus Maximus at Aquileia, he came to Milan there to receive a report from the Count of the East that at Callinicum, a fort in Mesopotamia, a synagogue had been burnt down in a riot stirred up by the local bishop; moreover, a conventicle of the Valentinian gnostics in the East had also been burnt by zealous monks, whose procession in honour of the Maccabaean martyrs had been mocked by the imprudent heretics. Theodosius directed that restitution be made, especially to the synagogue which the local bishop must rebuild. Ambrose of Milan thought it grave that the emperor should enable the Jews so to triumph over the church, and recalled the number of churches destroyed by Jewish rioters. His letter of protest made the emperor withdraw his order, though without informing Ambrose. On the next occasion when Ambrose was celebrating mass with the emperor present, he preached a pointed sermon on the prophetic duty to rebuke and on the courage of the prophet Nathan before king David. Descending from the ambo, Ambrose stood within the presbytery, and an irritated dialogue with the emperor ensued: "You have been preaching at me today." "True, I had your edification in view." "My decree that the bishop must restore the synagogue was too harsh; but it is already withdrawn. Yet the monks commit many crimes." ... After standing for some time Ambrose said to the emperor: "Enable me to offer for you without anxiety, set my mind at rest." Eventually the emperor gave his promise to quash the entire investigation by the Count of the East. "On your promise," said Ambrose, "I will celebrate mass (*ago*)." So he went to the altar at last and, as he reported to his sister, "so great was the grace of the offering that I myself felt that this grace was well pleasing to our God and that the divine presence was not lacking" (Ambrose, *Ep.* 41, 27-28).

The scene is a dramatic enforcement of the point that Ambrose cannot continue with the offering of the mass unless the emperor removes any ground for fear that the church in Mesopotamia may be harassed by the Count. For any such harassment would negative any value that the liturgy might possess in preserving the favour of heaven.

The role of the bishop as protector of the poor made him the natural leader of a large proportion of the urban population, and therefore a figure of political consequence. Particularly intolerant bishops seem to have been markedly unpopular. The terrible lynching of George of Alexandria when the news of Constantius' death reached the city in 361 shows the hatred that could be aroused by a bishop who enraged the pagans by his scorn for their religion.[17] At Arethusa in Syria the Arian bishop Mark died a heroic death at the hands of a fanatical mob resentful of his anti-pagan measures (Socrates 5, 10). A number of other texts could be added concerning the unpopularity of some individual bishops. But in general the bishop was a figure that people wanted to like, and of whom they hoped that their expectations would be realised. The pagan historian Ammianus Marcellinus regarded the church as a body concerned for justice, mercy, and simplicity (XXII 11, 5; XXVII 3, 15). It is noteworthy that his comments occur in passages criticising bishops conspicuously failing to realise these ideals. Ammianus was also aware that theological disputes within the Christian family could be contentious to the point of almost animal ferocity (XXII 5,4). (The Church's character as a universalised Judaism has somehow carried over a trait that Jews often remark about their own society, that they quarrel loudly among themselves, but are quickly united by external threats.) But Ammianus much admired the frugality of country bishops. His cordial dislike of anything associated with the city of Rome assigned a prominent place to Damasus (Pope 366-384), whose opulent hospitality was said to surpass the emperor's.

The public insignia assumed by bishops are relevant to their social role.[18] Before the time of Constantine Christian clergy wore no distinctive dress. The *Apostolic Constitutions* (VIII 12) direct that, as the liturgy of the faithful begins, the bishop celebrating is to put on a "shining garment." But otherwise the bishops normally, for everyday wear, dressed themselves in peasant black, no doubt as a sign of identification with the poor. At the end of the fourth century a witty Novatianist bishop of Constantinople wore white; but that was not his only eccentricity (Socrates VI 22). As early as the time of Constantine zealous believers in Phrygia took to

---

[17]George of Alexandria's death followed the fall of the hated *dux Aegypti* Artemius: *Historia Acephala* 8 (Turner, *EOMIA* I 666); Ammianus XXII 11, 8; Libanius, *Or.* 14, 65; *Ep.* 205; Julian, *Ep.* 10.

[18]T. Klauser, *Der Ursprung der bischöflichen Insignien und Ehrenrechte* (1949), now reprinted in his *Gesammelte Arbeiten* (1974).

wearing sackcloth. An inscription records Severus, bishop of Laodicea Combusta, as "general bishop of several cities and leader of the sackcloth-wearing people" (*MAMA* i 171). But sackcloth came to be regarded as the sign either of exceptional holiness (the emperor Theodosius II acquired for its sanctity a filthy black cassock left by a bishop of Hebron: Socrates VII 22, 14) or of ostentation (Cassian, *Inst.* I 2). To wear sackcloth became the mark of ecclesiastical dissent in Asia Minor (*C.Th.* XVI 5,7,9,11; 381-383).

Marks of public respect were normally paid to a bishop. Socrates the historian observes that he may give offence to ultra-zealots by omitting honorific epithets such as "God-beloved" (*theophilestatos*) which were commonly applied to bishops in formal chancery style (VI pr.). He also tells us in passing that it was customary to stand when a bishop came into the room (VI 11, 16). But an acid passage in Jerome's commentary on St. Matthew xxi commenting adversely on the practice of saluting bishops with the acclamation "Blessed is he that comes in the name of the Lord, Hosanna in the highest" has mistakenly been taken as a general observation about a widespread practice of using this acclamation at the advent of the bishop. The travel diary of Etheria gives reason to think it only a snide hit at the bishop of Jerusalem (with whom Jerome's relations were always tense) who reenacted the triumphal entry of Jesus by riding into town on a donkey in Holy Week. One may not generalise from something that happened once a year in one place.

The principal critics of bishops and their developing social role were the monks. "Flee from women and bishops" was an early monastic maxim reported by John Cassian (*Inst.* XI 18), who adds that he never kept away from his sister and had been ordained by a bishop (John Chrysostom, no less). But he understood the point of the saying to be that the monk's prime duty is unremitting concentration in prayer in the solitude of his cell, and to that end neither bishops nor women are conducive. The canons of the council of Gangra (about 342) show how in Asia Minor the monastic movement had taken on a sharply critical turn in relation to the church. The Egyptian *Apophthegmata Patrum* do not reflect any such anti-clericalism, and that is one of the more interesting features of these sayings. One monk who left his cell to become bishop of Oxyrhyncus tried, as bishop, to continue his monastic exercises as before, and found he lacked the strength. He asked the Lord if grace had been removed from him because of his accepting the bishopric and was told, No (*PG* 65, 133). But in Egypt Athanasius of Alexandria had fully identified himself with the ascetic movement, had written a *Life* of Antony to show how devoted that holy man had been to orthodoxy, and had gone up the Nile on a solemn visitation of the Pachomian foundations.[19]

There is no doubt that independent ascetics were felt by bishops to be disorderly persons (Origen, *in Matt.* 16, 25 says so explicitly). The Origenist tradition, with its anticlerical high churchmanship, adopted a detached, even scornful view of

---

[19]On the political consequences of Athanasius' achievement in winning the solid support of the monks there is direct evidence in Sozomen VI 20. On the tensions between monks and "secular" clergy cf. Jerome, *Ep.* 14, 8-9, and much other fourth-century evidence, especially in the *Apostolic Constitutions*, composed in part to emphasise in the strongest terms the authority of the bishop and his clergy against ascetic indifference. Likewise the pseudo-Ignatian epistles by the same author.

The role of the bishop in the ancient city receives notice in the recent studies of the ancient and medieval city by Mason Hammond. See also F. Prinz, "Die bischöfliche Stadtherrschaft in Frankreich vom 5. bis zum 7. Jht.," *Hist. Zeits.* 217 (1973) 1ff. and the same author's *Klerus und Krieg im frühen Mittelalter* (Stuttgart 1971). There is also a recent study of late antique Gaul's bishops by M. Heinzelmann.

popular worldly clerics, preaching eartickling sermons, favoured by ladies of wealth and refinement, easygoing with sinners in their congregation for fear of unpopularity (Origen, *H. Ezech.* 3, 3; *c. Cels.* III 9; *H. Jos.* 7, 6). Origen felt acutely the scandal caused by clergy of poor quality who were, he felt, a major hindrance to faith (*H. Ezech.* 7, 3). Men blaspheme and say, What a bishop! (*H. Num.* 2, 1). But congregations have the clergy they deserve (*H. Jud.* 4, 3). Augustine likewise remarks that worldly clergy are more popular than unworldly (*Ep.* 21, cf. S 26). The problem arose in part from the fact that so many run to the church for temporal aid rather than for eternal life (Augustine *en. ps.* 46, 5), and then complain that only widows and old women fill the churches (*S. Denis* 18, 6).

The ascetics went out into the desert because they felt themselves to be suffocated by the worldliness of the church in the towns (so John Chrysostom, *H. Eph.* VI; cf. John Cassian, *Coll.* 18, 5-7). The urban churches seemed so cultured and respectable, no longer identified with the poor and homeless except as the distributor of welfare. The financial resources of the church were increasingly channelled into buildings adorned with noble mosaics and frescoes. Constantine and his mother had lavished benefactions on the churches in the Holy Land and in Rome, had financed the production of exquisite calligraphic codices of the Bible, and had used a substantial part of the estates taken from Licinius to provide permanent endowments for the maintenance of their new buildings. A rich man might build a splendid church and then seem a natural candidate for election to the bishopric. The magnificent mosaic floor of the church at Aquileia records the munificence of the founder, bishop Theodore (314-320): *Theodore feli(x) (a)diuuante deo omnipotente et poemnio caelitus tibi (cre)ditum omnia (b)aeate fecisti et gloriose dedicasti* (*ILCV* 1863; van der Meer and Mohrmann, *Atlas of the Early Christian World*, pl. 140). At Laodicea Combusta in Phrygia the successor of the sackcloth-wearing Severus, Julius Eugenius, held the see for 25 years during which he "rebuilt the entire church from its foundations [to which it had been razed during the Diocletianic persecution] and all the adornment round it, i.e. with *stoai* and a *tetrastoa* and paintings and mosaics and a fountain and outer gateway and all the stone work and, in a word, with everything" (*MAMA* i 170). A century later at Kyrrhos bishop Theodoret used the revenues of his church (whose shrine of Cosmas and Damian attracted pilgrims and therefore had extra sources of income) to give dignity to the small and remote town; he built porticos, baths, two large bridges, and an aqueduct (*Epp.* 79, 81, 139 ed. Azema). Yet Theodoret was an ascetic, trained with and in the Syrian monastic milieu, and despite his high literary culture and easy contacts with those in high places writing his "History of God's Friends" (*Philotheos Historia*) to describe the great holy men of Syria such as Symeon Stylites in terms of unreserved admiration.

Theodoret of Kyrrhos could write as cultivated and "literary" a letter as anyone of the fifth century. He combines in himself many of the paradoxes of the church of his time in siding wholly with the illiterate hermits of the desert against the pagan literati. He also illustrates how much a public-spirited bishop could do for his town. There was not much reason to encourage cities of the later Roman Empire to feel a great deal of self-respect unless they had an imperial residence or enjoyed the dignity of being a metropolis. Nicaea and Nicomedia competed with one another in blowing their civic trumpet. But small towns in the provinces can only have been irretrievably dull and undistinguished. The church with its leader could impart a sense of significance to the civic community, especially if its church possessed the relics of a martyr or other holy man.

The relationship between bishops and pagan philosophers was on the whole distant. The church and the pagan philosophers agreed that what is required of man is to practise virtue, to contemplate the divine, and to become like God as far as possible.

They disagreed about polytheistic worship, especially the veneration of the Sun-God, and about the authority attaching to the wisdom and culture of classical Hellenism. At the public and social level, bishops and philosophers could sometimes look like rivals for the following of the people, or for the influencing of high officials. Both tended to come forward when the administration was in trouble with the people. But in general the bishops were, like the monks, identified with a community which included many individuals of high culture but was not as such a body intended for the diffusion of high culture and indeed often regarded high culture as aristocratic and elitist. The formidable strength of the church lay in its combination of insistence on the transcendent and supernatural together with the assumption that the church answers to the aspirations of ordinary mortals. The sense of rivalry can be illustrated from the legendary story told by Rufinus about the council of Nicaea in 325. There, he says (*H.E.* X 3 p. 962), the assembled bishops were confronted by clever philosophers skilled in dialectic who engaged the bishops in controversy, an *ingens spectaculum* for everyone to see and hear. One bishop of small education, who had courageously confessed his faith in the Persecution, asked leave to speak to a philosopher scornfully insulting the faith. The cultivated bishops present were embarrassed for their cause to be represented by such *sancta simplicitas*. (One recalls the direction of the *Didascalia* iii 5 that those enrolled as widows should not think themselves entitled to answer questions about the incarnation and atonement, but only about righteousness and simple faith.) But the good bishop stood his ground and stated his faith to the philosopher: that one God created heaven and earth by his Word and Wisdom, which Word and Wisdom was born of a virgin, by his passion freed man from eternal death, and will come as our Judge. Such was the power of the simple bishop's conviction that the philosopher found himself assenting and was carried off by the bishop to baptism. The point of Rufinus' story is that the kingdom of God is not in word but in power; that the authority of the bishop does not reside in internal qualities of mind or natural ability, but in the word of God entrusted to the church; that the bishop's right to be listened to lies in his being the successor of God's fishermen. He was not a gentleman, but "an inspired cad, like the apostles."

The Christianisation of the Roman empire meant, in short, the emergence of a new type of leader within the community, chosen (at least in the early period) by the local church, but through his consecration by bishops from other churches also linked to a world-wide society, and, unless he fell into heresy or resigned to become a monk, enjoying permanent tenure for life. His role was guided by rules formulated within the Christian tradition. He supremely represented the unity and continuity of the Christian society, and by the commission of his ordination combined both an institutional authority and charismatic power. The Roman government had no experience at coping with the phenomenon. The emperors tried to harness the bishops to social purposes by assimilating them to magistrates, by fostering their charitable welfare, and in times of war or political crisis by using their independence and "neutrality" for complex negotiations.

Response by Peter Brown, Professor of Classics and of History
University of California, Berkeley

In this paper, Henry Chadwick has delineated for us the role of the Christian bishop in ancient society with all the fineness of line and sense of perspective of a Dürer engraving. So perceptive a mobilization of so much out-of-the-way evidence makes us realize how much there is still to be learned about the quality of life in the ancient world in general from the voluminous, and frequently shameless, evidence for the life of the Christian church, and how much we stand to lose in our understanding of the Christian church itself, if we content ourselves with neat compartmentations separating history from theology, ecclesiastical institutions from Late Roman society, the classical world from Late Antiquity, and the period of the Early Church from that of the post-Constantinian establishment. It is also a reminder, in its loving and patient erudition, that sociological speculation on the role of Christianity in society, in any period, laudable and topical though this may be, can proceed with 'liberating precision' only if nourished, as in the manner of this paper, on respect for the irreducible, almost surrealist, particularity of the surviving evidence of life lived twenty-four hours a day in a world very different from our own.

On reading this masterly and original presentation, it seems to me that we have come much closer to understanding an aspect of the later phases of the ancient world which has challenged scholars since the time of Gibbon--the *novelty* of the type of authority exercised in ancient society by the Christian bishop, in particular, and the Christian clergy, in general. It is on this aspect of Henry Chadwick's paper that I would wish to concentrate.

For like all successful revolutions, the rise of the Christian church has made it difficult to catch the precise flavor of the novelty of the bishop's position. Fifteen hundred years of bishops, good, bad and indifferent, now stand between us and the ancient world in which they first appeared. It has become an integral part of our culture to assume that we know what we mean when we talk about such phenomena as 'episcopal authority' of processes such as 'the establishment of the church' and 'the growth of worldliness,' of motivations such as 'clerical ambition' and of activities such as 'the relief of the poor' or 'the acceptance of women.' The phrases have become far more for us than labels: each assumes a chain of cause and effect, whose links are taken as understood--'the establishment of the church' is linked to 'a growth of worldliness,' and the responses which this in turn evoked seem eminently explicable; 'relief of the poor' and 'the acceptance of women' seems obviously linked to 'the spread of Christianity.' The phenomena seem connected with all the inevitability of physical laws of motion. Yet the very freshness and vividness of the evidence presented in this paper encourages us to step back, for a moment, behind the language that we conventionally use to describe the rise of the Christian church and the articulation of its institutions, into a world where this language had not taken on a patina of the obvious. Ancient men, in the period covered by Henry Chadwick, were frequently at a loss for words to describe the institution that had arisen in their midst. Usually, they used words heavy with value-judgment *sub specie aeternitatis*. Yet these value judgments often betray the specific preoccupations of ancient men in an ancient society. Put briefly: even among the clergy, the ravages of original sin are historically determined; and those accusations of 'ambition,' 'arrogance,' 'toadyism' and 'worldliness' which liberally punctuate contemporary accounts of the rise of the Christian bishop into an outstanding position in Late Roman society--and that survive in many modern accounts of the process--each of them refer to specifically Late Roman versions of these vices, and are as little to be taken for granted by being confused with their medieval and modern counterparts, as are the equally particular flavor of Late Roman courage, conscientiousness and sanctity for which this paper also provides impressive testimony. Part of the problem facing the historian of the Early Christian church is not merely to free the development of Christianity from confessional or anti-confessional value-judgments: it is to translate a process which was, indeed, fraught with sufficient tensions and ambiguities to arouse comment not only among Christians, but among pagans also--one would, for instance, have liked to attend those *operas Bouffes* performed in the fourth century by pagan repertory companies on the theme of Christian baptism or on Christian theological controversy[1]--back from the level of moral judgment into the precise sociological ambiguities in the role of the bishop in ancient society that made such judgments inevitable but unrevealing. Only then will we have freed the history of the Early Church from that aura of false familiarity into which it slips only too easily once we move from the known alien-ness of its theology to discuss the seemingly more 'practical,' and consequently more accustomed, problems of its concrete impact on the world.

For what seems to me to emerge most clearly from Chadwick's paper, is that from the first century A.D. onwards, groups living in face-to-face societies that had arranged their religious and political affairs very differently, and would continue to do so as Jews and pagans, decided to place themselves, in religious matters, under the life-long leadership of one man and his colleagues; that the choice involved a degree of participation on the part of the interested group which, although it had parallels in ancient decision-making, had rarely been used to place one man, chosen by his merits, in an irreversible position of leadership at the urban level; that an influential proportion of the participants in this decision, and in the consequent accountancy that such a decision could precipitate, were drawn from categories that had little or no previous existence on an ancient man's map of his political world--the poor and the women; and that this decision-making was brought to bear to produce leadership of the group on a range of issues far wider than the purely cultic--the patronage of the bishop was not an accidental accretion to his original position: it reflected a willingness on the part of the Christian group to allow him and his clergy to play a crucial role in the re-distribution of wealth and the resolution of litigation. As a result, the 'chemistry' of a bishop's authority was, by ancient standards, a new and potentially explosive compound. Much of the institutional history of the Christian church in Late Antiquity is best seen, not in terms of an inevitable progression, but as so many temporary attempts, differing profoundly from time to time and from region to region, to give the new compound stability by adjusting the proportions of its elements. While, far from being explicable in sweeping moral terms, as a process of decline from the purity of the Early Church to the worldliness and 'triumphalism' of the post-Constantinian *Reichskirche*, the course of ecclesiastical history is that of an institution struggling to contain potentially explosive elements placed in the heart of its structures.

To begin with, it is amazing that we know so much about the Christian bishops from a comparatively early period. This in itself is a breach of the rules for the exercise of authority in the ancient world. Our 'evidence' for such exercise of authority had been drawn almost totally from the upper classes. Paul Veyne, *Le pain et le Cirque* (Paris 1976) and Ramsay MacMullen, *Roman Social Relations* (Yale U.P. 1974) have made plain the mechanisms by which the aristocracies of the Hellenistic and Roman worlds had concentrated to themselves not only an almost total monopoly of real power, but also the ability to explain and record the political process. The 'grass roots' politics of lesser men, in their towns, in their *quartiers* and in their associations, survives only as so many vivid but tantalising fragments. All that we can say is that

---

[1]G.J. Theocharides, *Beiträge zur Geschichte des byzantinischen Profantheaters im IV. und V. Jht.* (Thessalonica 1940) 69, 95-101.

it happened and happened vigorously.[2] As a result, attempts to judge the role of the Christian church in Roman society from the first century onwards has been largely frustrated, not because the Christian evidence is slender, but because evidence of a similar quality for the non-aristocratic majority of the Roman world is, by comparison, almost non-existent. Compared, for instance, with the flamboyant rise to power in the Roman community of a man like bishop Callistus, as this is told with withering precision by Hippolytus,[3] his contemporaries, the worthies who had risen to local dignity through the corporations connected with the *annona* services in Ostia, though plainly active men in a complex situation, are no more than names on inscriptions for us.[4] One ancient historian, who shall be nameless, was heard to remark that "The Acts of the Apostles are footnotes to history; they are not history." For the social historian it is the other way round: the social history of the Roman Empire in the classical period--and that includes the concrete conditions of the exercise of power--will make progress only if we can see all its inhabitants with the same precision and *sans gêne* as they are seen in early Christian sources.

The vividness of the Christian evidence itself points to a social phenomenon of some importance. The Christian church addressed audiences that were less fastidious about what they wished to record. The marvellous richness of the evidence collected by Chadwick reflects that 'democratization of culture' which has long been regarded as one of the most important features of late antique civilisation, and of the role of Christianity within it.[5] Yet 'democratization' in itself does not quite explain the phenomenon. For what is being washed in public before an ever-widening audience is so frequently dirty linen: vivid vignettes of bishops in action recorded by rivals and critics. We know as much as we do about the tentacular social influence of the Christian bishop, generations before the conversion of Constantine, because for one Christian bishop or clergyman, there is usually another Christian polemist or colleague for whom "to tell the truth was not only a duty but a pleasure."[6] A significant

---

[2]See especially Lellia Cracco Ruggini, "Le associazioni professionali nel mondo romano-bizantino," *Settimana di studio del centro di studi sull' alto medioevo* 18 (1970) 59-227; "La vita associativa nelle città dell' oriente greco," *Assimilation et résistance à la culture grêco-romaine dans le monde ancien*, ed. D.M. Pippidi (Bucharest 1976) 464-491; "*Collegium* e *corpus*: la politica economica nella legislazione e nella prassi," *Circolo toscano di diritto romano e storia del diritto* 4 (1976) 63-94.

[3]Hippolytus, *Refutatio* IX.12: see H. Gülzow, "Kallist von Rom. Ein Beitrag zur Soziologie der römischen Gemeinde," *Zeitschrift der neutestamentl. Wiss.* 58 (1959) 102-121.

[4]R.E. Lyast, "O sostave i politicheskoi roli korporatsii sviazannich so sluzhbami annoni v Ostii" ("The composition and political role of the corporations connected with the annona services in Ostia"), *Vestnik drevnei istorii* 112 (1970) 149-161, is a conscientious study.

[5]Santo Mazzarino, "La democratizzazione della cultura nel basso impero," *Rapports du XIème congrés des sciences historiques* (Stockholm 1960) 235-254 and *The End of the Ancient World* (London 1966) 159-165; Ramsay MacMullen, *Enemies of the Roman Order* (Cambridge, Mass. 1967) 192-268 and "A note on *sermo humilis*," *Journal of Theological Studies* 17 (1966) 108-112; and Peter Brown, "Christianity and Local Culture in Late Roman Africa," *Journal of Roman Studies* 58 (1968) 85-95 = *Religion and Society in the Age of Saint Augustine* (London 1972) 279-300.

[6]E.g. the declarations of the bishops on Paul of Samosata in Eusebius, *Hist. Eccles.* VII.30.8-9 as now commented by Fergus Millar, "Paul of Samosata, Zenobia and Aurelian: the church, local culture and political allegiance in the third century," *Journal of Roman Studies* 61 (1971) 1-17.

proportion of the evidence marshalled by Chadwick comes from polemical statements or refers to situations of crisis. This, in itself, is a measure of the novelty of the bishop's position. His authority involved so many elements, and its exercise touched on so many interests, that no bishop could hope to get his mixture entirely right, to the satisfaction of all observers. We know far less about the tensions of pagan priesthoods because the 'chemistry' of their authority was usually less complex: their authority in most regions was less far-reaching and, even more so, access to and the exercise of this authority does not seem to have required such wide-ranging, circumstantial and frequent social accountancy. The ideal chemistry of the authority of the bishop was so subtle an essence as to exist to a large extent in the eye of the beholder; and so we know as much as we do about it because so many beholders, on so many occasions, refused to view with rosy-tinted spectacles particular cases of access to and the exercise of this ideal authority by particular individuals. "Happy is the priesthood without a history" could be said more convincingly of the pagan than of the Christian world.

For, by ancient standards, Henry Chadwick presents us with a *monstrum*: a man who "by the commission of his ordination combined both an institutional authority and charismatic power" (p. 14). To ancient men, this delicate combination of what one might call 'achieved status' with 'vested power,' confirmed at crucial moments by the agreement of human agents, was an attempt to square the circle. It existed most clearly at a safe distance--in the person of the Emperor. It had rarely been brought into the political arena of the cities. Here, parallels for the decision-making processes that went into the election of the bishop, and that coloured the nature of his role, are numerous; but they are never combined in the same way. Thus: the excited scenes that often culminated in the 'gentle violence' of forcible ordination to the priesthood or the episcopate, which strike a modern reader as so strange, were an entirely acceptable application of normal procedures for the distribution of administrative burdens among members of the urban upper classes.[7] Popular participation might even reach the level of a charivari, constraining the magnates to shoulder the burdens that they owed the town.[8] Imperial governors, also, were subject to the pressure of public opinion, skillfully mobilised in the form of acclamations at the theatre and circus.[9] Yet this popular participation was brought to bear either to decide on the alternations of power and responsibility from among a group of men of 'ascribed status'--all members of the town councils--or, in the case of Imperial governors, to temper the exercise of authority by equally transitory representatives of the central government. At no time--with the significant exception of the Emperor--was it supposed to lodge a man in a position of permanent authority. As Gibbon wrote:

> these absolute monarchs respected the freedom of ecclesiastical elections, and, while they distributed and resumed the honours of the state and army, they allowed eighteen hundred perpetual magistrates to receive their important offices from the free suffrages of the people.[10]

---

[7]E.g. Pap. Rylands II, 77 in Grenfell and Hunt, *Select Papyri* II, no. 241.

[8]E.g. Bücheler, *Carmina latina epigraphica: Anthologia Latina* (Leipzig 1895) no. 417.

[9]E.g. W. Liebeschütz, *Antioch* (Oxford 1972) 209-217 and Alan Cameron, *Circus Factions* (Oxford 1976) 237-244.

[10]Edward Gibbon, *Decline and Fall of the Roman Empire*, ch. xx.

No matter how ingeniously this situation might be modified to the detriment of the 'free suffrages of the people,' the original instability of the compound remained. For popular participation, though usually peripheral, condensed an ineradicable element in the bishop's position. Even in the most securely Christianised and stable provinces of the Late Roman world, the episcopate never became an 'ascribed status.'[11] Priesthood and episcopate alike carried with them the heady flavor of 'achieved status.' At one time or other, a bishop or priest had to 'rise' to his office on his 'merits' (or be thought to have done so), and would often be called upon to justify his authority in terms of his personal religious and social achievements. Once again, Gibbon put this elegantly:

> The children of the (pagan) priests enjoyed, with proud and indolent security, their sacred inheritance; and the fiery spirit of enthusiasm was abated by the cares, the pleasures and the endearments of domestic life. But the Christian sanctuary was open to every ambitious candidate who aspired to its heavenly promises or temporal possessions.[12]

Ambitio, a term to which ancient men were hypersensitive, was written into the constitution of the Christian church. We have only to compare this situation with the meticulous ritual control of upward-mobility which Richard Gordon has stressed in his admirable new studies of Mithraism,[13] or with the occasional wistful glance which Christians cast in the direction of the imperial bureaucracy, with its enviable system of smooth promotion by seniority alone,[14] to realise the extent to which Christian institutions were novel and troubling to contemporaries. *Ambitio*, *adfectatio*, *adrogantia*, and *opulentia*, in their strict Late Roman connotations, should not be regarded as individual sins which individual bishops committed by departing from the original simplicity of the Christian religion, nor as symptoms of a denaturing of the original structures of the Early Church by the establishment of the Imperial *Reichskirche*. Such neat moral judgments, to which pagan and Christian contemporaries frequently resorted, mask the deeper dilemma. The Christian church would have ceased to be what it was if these tensions had not been part of the peculiar logic of its institutions. The conversion of Constantine and the establishment of Christianity is not an important turning point in the unfolding of this logic. As P. Nautin has said, clearly and rightly:

> The conversion of Constantine and the entry of the bishops into the life of the imperial court did not modify the life of the Christian church as deeply as one might think. When we find in the Church styles of life and action that shock our modern aspirations, we tend to say that these were the consequence of what we call 'Caesaro-papism.' How much we have written in this vein since the last Council (Vatican II)! We should realise that this apologetic interpretation bears no relation to history. No: the fault is not Constantine's. The structures, the ways of thinking, the patterns of behaviour which we have described all go back before the fourth century.[15]

---

[11]Peter Brown, *Relics and Social Status in the Age of Gregory of Tours* (University of Reading 1977) 17-20.

[12]Gibbon, *Decline and Fall*, ch. xx.

[13]R.L. Gordon, "Mithraism and Roman Society," *Religion* 2 (1972) 92-121, esp. p. 108.

[14]Zosimus, *Ep.* 9,1.

[15]P. Nautin, "L'évolution des ministères au iie et au iiie siècles," *Revue de droit canonique* 23 (1973) 57.

The novelty of the position of the bishop was made clear not only in the manner of his access to power, but in the unexpected nature of the groups with which he had a special relation. We are only beginning to appreciate the extent to which a relationship with the poor, as such, existed only on the margins of an ancient man's view of his society; and that the role of Christianity cannot be reduced merely to its charitable activities among the poor--it enabled a whole society to perceive the poor in the first place. The studies of Paul Veyne and Evelyne Patlagean have now shown how one of the principal changes from a classical to a post-classical society was the replacement of a particularised political model of society, in which the unit was the city, its composition a particularised political model of society, in which the unitwas the city, its composition defined in terms of citizens and non-citizens, by the more all-embracing, economic model, in which society as a whole (that is, city and country alike) was seen as divided between the 'rich' and the 'poor,' the rich having a duty of support the poor expressed in strictly religious terms as almsgiving.[16] It is also clear both that this model of society spread largely from the Christian communities outwards, and that its spread both coincided with and facilitated profound changes in the social and economic structure of the late antique city and of its relationship to the surrounding countryside.

In a society where membership of the community was expressed most clearly in terms of the patron-client relationship,[17] and where the giving of gifts (money, clothing, food and entertainment) was the traditional symbol of this relationship, the care of the poor by the Christian bishop was far more than a laudable form of economic relief for the distressed which others might equally well have performed. It re-drew the boundaries of the Late Roman urban community, and it placed the bishop at the symbolic centre of an entirely new circle embracing a new category of participants. As the *Canons of Athanasius* of the Coptic Church said, with engaging candour:

> This word have we spoken concerning the poor; God has established the bishop because of the feasts, that he may refresh them at the feasts ...[18]

Hence the dramatic impact of Imperial support after the conversion of Constantine; within a few years, the Christian bishop as almsgiver moved from a world of 'conventional' weapons into a 'thermo-nuclear' age of gift-giving.[19] The famous remark of Donatus of Carthage, "What has the emperor to do with the church" referred specifically to this crisis: by distributing funds either to his rivals or directly to the Christian poor, imperial commissioners were robbing him of something more than his popularity--they threatened to undermine the symbolic position of the bishop as the unique center of a new cycle of the redistribution of wealth.[20]

Furthermore, not all 'non-citizens' were poor. In a characteristically erudite and perceptive survey, Lellia Cracco Ruggini has pointed out that, by the late fourth

---

[16]Paul Veyne, *Le Pain et le Cirque* 45-66; Evelyne Patlagean, *Pauvreté économique et pauvreté sociale à Byzance* (Paris 1977) 17-35.

[17]Tacitus, *Historiae* 1.4: see Veyne, *Le Pain* 696.

[18]Pseudo-Athanasius, canon 16, cited in E. Wipszicka, *Les ressources et les activités économiques de l'église en Égypte* (Brussels 1972) 110.

[19]Cf. Augustine, *Ad catholicos ep.* 25.73; Eusebius, *Hist. Eccles.* X.6 (400 *folles* vs. 3000 *folles*); and C. Pietri, *Roma christiana* (Paris 1977) I.84 (553 kilograms vs. 3.7 tons of silver and one-third kilo vs. 500 kilograms of gold, the larger gift in each case given by Constantine).

[20]Optatus of Milevis, *De schismate Donatistarum* III.3.

century, the Christian bishop seems to have enjoyed particularly close links with the *corpora* of traders and skilled artisans, such as the vital colonies of armament-makers scattered along the imperial roads of Asia Minor and the Balkans.[21] These were often immigrants to the city. Thus, as patron to the newly defined community, the Christian bishop was far from having a *clientela* limited to the economically impotent: he enjoyed a special relationship, as protector of strangers, to just those bodies of men on whom the economic structures of the late antique city depended. The young Augustine was not the only enterprising and potentially influential *peregrinus* whom Ambrose was able to absorb into Milan, *satis episcopaliter.*[22]

It is the same with the women. When Ambrose was a little boy, he played at being a bishop. Significantly, this took the form of offering his hand to be kissed by the *women* of the household.[23] For the first time, with the formal duty of the bishop as protector of widows and the unmarried, and in the ceremonial of giving the veil to consecrated virgins, we have a political *clientela* that explicitly included members of the other sex. To become a bishop meant stepping out of the all-male world of traditional politics, to become *patronus* of women as well as of men. Some hated it. In becoming bishop of Ptolemais, the philosopher Synesius came up against a new, intractable element, not easily manipulated by discreet man to man stratagems:

> the women, who are proverbially difficult to control, lifted their arms, they raised their infants towards Heaven, they closed their eyes that they might not see the bishop's seat ...[24]

Others feared it. Monastic disapproval of episcopal and priestly ambition was very often a disapproval for men whose *clientela* was made up from a dangerous and novel admixture of the sexes. Such anomalous mixtures had been more current in the mixed society of women and eunuchs at the imperial court than in the provinces.[25] Yet we see how the bishops of the major cities acted as impresarios for the piety of their female clients, thus giving to senatorial and Imperial women a public role which they had lacked. As benefactors of the poor and as builders they became participants in a ceremonial life from which they had largely been excluded in the all-male definition of the city as a political unit. Thus, in fourth-century Rome, senatorial heiresses of great wealth and inestimable if intangible influence were still studiously denied a role in the public life of the city. As an edict pointed out, they might pay for the games given by their dead husbands or fatherless sons, but it would be 'out of place and shameful' if they were to appear on such occasions in the male insignia of the senatorial order: plainly they needed to be told their place.[26] Bishops had less hesitation. The intangible influence of women was publicly registered and orchestrated in the newly-defined Christian community--and usually in relation to the other new participants, the poor. The admirable study of Ken Holum on the role played by the public piety of

---

[21]L. Cracco Ruggini, "Le associazioni professionali ..." 167 n. 212 and 171.

[22]Augustine, *Confessions* V.xiii,23.

[23]Paulinus of Milan, *Vita Ambrosii* 4.

[24]Synesius of Cyrene, *Ep.* 67.

[25]K.M. Hopkins, "Eunuchs in politics in the Later Roman Empire," *Proc. Cambridge Philol. Society* 189 (1963) 62-80 ; cf. Socrates, *Hist. Eccles.* II, 2.

[26]*Codex Theodosianus* VI.4.17 ; see Santo Mazzarino, *End of the Ancient World* 131-132.

Pulcheria at the court of Theodosius II shows how, without the cooperation of the Christian clergy, the women of the Imperial family, on whom the hopes of an orthodox dynasty depended, would have enjoyed no formal status in the public life of the new capital.[27]

In pages of characteristic sanity, Arnaldo Momigliano has said:

> Much can be said about the internal conflicts, the worldly ambitions, the intolerance of the Church. Yet the conclusion remains that while the political organization of the Empire became increasingly rigid, unimaginative, and unsuccessful, the Church was mobile and resilient and provided space for those whom the State was unable to absorb.[28]

Henry Chadwick's admirable paper now makes plain that this could not have happened if, from its earliest centuries, the Christian communities had not made the imprudent and fertile decision to join forms of power, ways of access to this power and groups intimately concerned with its exercise which the long, slow wisdom of Mediterranean urban life had, up till then, chosen to keep apart.

---

[27]Kenneth C. Holum, "Pulcheria's Crusade A.D. 421-422 and the Ideology of Imperial Victory," *Greek, Roman and Byzantine Studies* 18 (1977) 153-172.

[28]A.D. Momigliano, "Introduction: Christianity and the Decline of the Roman Empire," *The Conflict Between Paganism and Christianity in the Fourth Century*, ed. A.D. Momigliano (Oxford 1963) 10,

Response by Dr. Robert M. Grant, Professor of Early Christian Literature
University of Chicago

It is difficult to add much to a paper so ably presenting so much evidence. All I have to present consists of two footnotes of unequal length. The first is on the idea of succession mentioned on page 1, and its implementation. Any organization needs to provide for orderly succession from one generation to another. This is so whether we deal with emperors, philosophers, high priests, or bishops. To limit the models for early Christians to either philosophers or high priests seems mistaken. The readers of the *Didache* are to understand that resident prophets are their high priests and they are to appoint bishops and deacons for the ministry of the prophets and teachers. The functions of the offices do not seem sharply differentiated. It is the Gnostic Ptolemaeus who speaks only of teaching handed down in the apostolic tradition by succession, and it may be that because of Irenaeus' anti-Ptolemaic stance he laid special emphasis on the same aspect of succession, referring to presbyter-bishops who "with the succession of the episcopate received the sure charisma of truth in accordance with the good pleasure of the Father" (*Adv. haer.* IV 26, 2; cf. 27, 1). While he also believed that as Christ performed the work of the high priest, so all his disciples were priests (IV 8, 2-3), he does not seem to have coordinated priesthood with succession. In Hippolytus, however, the fusion takes place (*Ref.* I, praef. 6). He refers to "the Holy Spirit handed down in the church" as a form of power "which the apostles formerly obtained and transmitted to orthodox believers." We are (or Hippolytus is) the successors of these apostles "since we share in the same gift of high priesthood and teaching." Here the two strands are united. The point may be theological, but it is certainly important for the conception of the bishop's authority within the church--as both high priest and teacher.

My second point is rather severely practical, and is related to Cyprian's view that "the episcopate ought to be unanimous" and "that decisions in synod are not reached by majority votes that preserve the conscientious dissent of the minority" (p. 4). It seems likely that one can learn something of the political mechanics of Cyprian's synods by examining the names preserved in relation to the 2nd, 4th, 5th, and 7th synods held from 251 to 256 at Carthage. The synodal letters and the *Sententiae episcoporum* naturally reveal procedural parallels with non-Christian assemblies. In addition, they can tell us something about the way in which a strong provincial leader (not yet a metropolitan *de jure*) could marshal and control his forces.

The first question to raise concerns the presence of steady and reliable support in the four synods for which we have names. Epistle 57 tells us about the second synod. Forty-two bishops were present, urging the readmission of penitents. Fifteen of these were stalwarts, attending the fourth (254), fifth (255), and seventh synods (256). Ten may not have cared to question decisions made at Rome and discussed in the later synods; their names do not reappear. Six would return for the fifth synod, on rebaptism, but not for the seventh. Six others would return for the fifth and the seventh. Four would come to the fourth but not to the fifth; then to the seventh. Only one would reappear only at the seventh. Thus out of the forty-two, nineteen had attended the second and would attend the seventh. Fifteen of these would also attend the fifth. Of the eighteen new attenders, only three would go to both the fifth and the seventh, and fourteen would reappear only at the seventh. One would drop out entirely. It looks as though some resistance to Cyprian's pressure had developed.

The fifth synod was attended by only thirty-one bishops, since it was to deal with questions raised by colleagues in Numidia (*Ep.* 70). Fifteen of them were fully reliable, having been present at the second and fourth synods and about to appear at the seventh. Three who had previously attended only the fourth would go on to the seventh, as would one new member. This gives a total of nineteen out of thirty-one.

The other twelve had previously been noted only at the second. Half of them would go on to the seventh, while half would drop out.

Finally we come to September 256 and the effort made to have eighty-seven bishops on hand. Forty-three seem to have been new; that is, we do not know that they attended earlier synods, though we may suspect that they swelled the attendance at the third synod (sixty-six bishops) and the sixth (seventy-one bishops). The core of Cyprian's support must have been found in the fifteen always present plus the thirteen earlier present at two and the sixteen only at one (of these, fourteen had spoken against Rome at the fourth synod).

It is fairly clear that old hands dominated the fourth synod and that some newcomers did not welcome their domination. The fifth synod was also controlled by the "regulars," though Cyprian's Numidian allies were absent. Numidians joined Africans at the sixth synod and reiterated what Cyprian wanted. The seventh synod was almost a mass demonstration in favor of the same view.

At this synod there were of course keynote speakers. The prominent bishop Caecilius (at other synods named 5th, 2nd, and 6th) spoke first. His views were reiterated by sixteen other bishops (numbers 2, 5, 14, 21, 22, 34, 36, 45, 46, 50, 55, 67, 68, 72, 73, and 80; note the occasional pairs). Obviously he was Cyprian's henchman. Close to the beginning came some of the Numidians, one of whom spoke at considerable length.

One might think it natural for the bishops to speak "by seniority," as E.W. Benson held (*DCB* I 750). Consideration of relatively uncommon (i.e., not duplicated) names shows that this is not the case. Take Sattius, 39th in 256 and 18-16-31 earlier, and compare him with similar examples:

Name	Rank	Relative Sequence			
Sattius	18-16-31-39	B	C	E	A
Pomponius	35-12-19-48	E	A	B	B
Rogatianus	15-23-26-60	A	D	D	C
Quintus	28-27-21-65	C	E	C	D
Honoratus	29-13-13-77	D	B	A	E

Thus seniority cannot be involved. Some people must be near the beginning or the end simply because they are reliable. Successus of Abbir Germaniciana is presumably placed (9-7-11-16) with Fortunatus of Thuccabori (11-9-14-17) for this reason. Junius of Neapolis comes just before Cyprian because he has been trustworthy in the past (6-absent-4-86).

The reason why position in expressing *sententiae* was so important was that the decision was being delivered, as Dean Chadwick notes, on the basis of consensus, not voting. Consensus, as under Lyndon Johnson, requires that the decision be made in advance of the meeting and the persuasive comments of powerful representatives are needed in order to remind participants what the party line is. Cyprian's address to the bishops at the seventh synod, "Each of us should bring forth what we think," means only that each should present some good reason for adhering to the consensus already achieved.

I do not feel capable of dealing with "methodological issues" in regard to what I have said. What informs my comments is observation of academic and ecclesiastical politics past and present, as well as some participation. Experience of this kind cannot very well be reduced to a book of rules, but it can suggest what may be going on.

Response by Dr. Ramsay MacMullen
Professor of History, Yale University

The role of the Christian bishop in ancient society touches so many other types of people and institutions, and takes on, by the fourth century, so much historical prominence, that it hardly permits a short description. Within a dozen pages or so, however, the job could not be better done than by Dr. Chadwick. Readers of those pages can only trace over again the broad outlines offered them, though perhaps bearing down and putting more weight on certain parts that strike them as too lightly drawn.

It is clearly right to begin with the authority of the bishop inside the Church, from which, at least formally, derived his force of intervention into affairs outside. And it is right, too, that the passion and bloodshed attending the election of Damasus in Rome or Timothy in Alexandria should receive mention, since of course the only position throughout the history of the Empire for which there was open, public competition, and some degree of participation of the masses in the outcome, was the episcopal. From the popular involvement in elections, *con amore* or with "almost animal ferocity" (as Dr. Chadwick paraphrases Ammianus), it is tempting to deduce, further, "that authority grows 'from the bottom upwards'," and that "the bishop's power-base, so to speak, lay always in the allegiance of his flock" (p. 5). Tempting, and in some sense correct. Yet shouting and yelling crowds of partisans in the large cities, and occasional outbursts of mass arson, vandalism and lynchings, are perhaps better taken as signs that the masses were really excluded from choice of all sorts, than that the later Empire (when such signs become more frequent) had somehow become more 'democratic.' It was only, or largely, because people felt themselves quite powerless in all normal ways that they resorted to the abnormal to express their wishes.

By pelting a man with stones, or burning his house down, or rampaging around his place of work or refuge, they certainly got his attention. If he had erred, he would try in future to do a lot better. Modern students of these phenomena cannot avoid concluding that the man in the streets of Antioch, Constantinople or Carthage, or more often in the hippodromes and amphitheaters of those centers, influenced events. But two remarks should be offered to correct any misapprehension: First, the expression of a general opinion by a great gathering took no institutional form. In the capital as in all other cities, there was no citizen assembly to be consulted.[1] Second, extreme expressions of some wish testify to the frustrating of that wish and probably many others as well for a long time prior. They had been pent up. Hence the force behind them when they could at last find an outlet. The two remarks together suggest that, through the death of 137 partisans of the other candidate in 366, the partisans of Damasus were showing a great deal more than their passionate advocacy of whatever their own man stood for (if anything). They were saying something about the nature of power in late antiquity, power which it was not usually their lot to touch, and barely to understand.

"It is hardly surprising that episcopal elections were normally a source of unrest and disorder," Dr. Chadwick tells us. To the subject of physical violence as an ingredient of power we will return. But no one supposes that ingredient to have been something necessary and essential to a bishop. The most recondite and pacific of

---

[1]Here I exclude various vestigial and quite meaningless civic assemblies for local electoral purposes. I also exclude the army, in which, aside from the well-known ceremony of Schilderhebung, formalities of consultation had always existed--Tacitus' *Histories* offer examples--and are referred to in the fourth century as *contiones* or the like (SHA *Maximini* 17.7; *Gordiani* 30.1; *Probus* 10.1).

abilities were valued in leaders both of the Church and of secular society, a fact needing no demonstration. To be able to see clearly through a complicated question and explain one's views in a fashion that made others want to agree and obey, was the gift possessed by many, many bishops, a gift moreover that implies some sort of resonance between them and their flock. Still, on occasion, a different source of suasion than pure reasoning is revealed, in the successful harangues of (for example) John Chrysostom *On the Statues*. In spoken form far more even than in their written form, they cannot have been readily understood by the average citizen of Antioch. Whence then derived their power? And when Libanius of Antioch describes someone as having "power" in the city, δύναμις, why does he attribute it to a person's "family, *culture* (λόγων), actions and liturgies" (*Ep.* 1393, Foerster XI 435)? The answer, I think, lies in the demonstration of membership in a class that people automatically deferred to, a class of the highly and very expensively educated who, as the man in the street might say, "talked funny, that's how you can tell he's really one of them." It went very much against the grain and indeed may have diminished such a person's effectiveness in public to indulge in plain speaking. Certainly it needed explanation: "I *could* speak like an Oxford or Harvard graduate, but excuse me for the moment ..."--such or similar apologies are common in literature of the Empire, secular or ecclesiastical.[2]

The Church must similarly struggle, in the end not at all successfully, against all the fancy show-off clothing worn by people high in the world. A very good judge of what was needed to enhance the authority of religious leaders writes, "I believe it behooves priests when they are serving to wear clothing the most impressive possible."[3] In the same fashion one might defend the special honorific titles won by bishops,[4] or at least explain the urgent desire to institute them. And Church leaders equally valued and "boasted of the front seat in their churches" and even at the taking of communion, "the falsely-termed *agape*,"[5] *proedria* being an honor instantly understood as setting a person apart from and above all the rest of the world. On the other hand, a ruler who put aside pompous manners would be criticized for behavior "unnatural and cheap."[6]

The setting in which the actual exertion or display of power would be the first visualized would be, I suppose, court hearings. There, one tried to establish one's place in the social hierarchy so as to benefit from the reception that respectable status might receive. The effort at display can be seen at various points in our only specimen of a defendant's oratory from the period of the Empire, Apuleius' *Apologia*. Apuleius wants to make clear by his culture (λόγων, to use Libanius' term) what class he belongs to. But a judge would have found it out anyway: "Zenophilus the governor said to Castus, 'What is your station in life?' Castus said, 'I have no rank'."[7] And Basil protests sharply at a judge accepting testimony from a witness who is without distinction.[8] Different social ranks entitled one to different sorts of hearing, even

[2]For a hint at the problem, see *Jnl.Theol.Stud.* 17 (1966) 111.

[3]Julian, *Letter to a Priest* 303B; for the broader background of display and ceremony across all ranks of society, see *Art Bull.* 46 (1964) 447f.

[4]T. Klauser, *Gesammelte Arbeiten* ... (1974) 198f.

[5]Clem. Alex., *Strom.* 7.16 (*PG* 9.536B).

[6]Ammianus 22.7.1, cf. Soc., *H.E.* 3.1.50 (= 172), though compare Ammianus' own views on the best manners for bishops, 27.3.15.

[7]Optatus, ed. Ziwsa (*CSEL* XXVI p. 195), the *Gesta apud Zenophilum.*

[8]Basil, *Ep.* 237, ἄσημος.

to different kinds of punishment or leniency spelt out in law.[9]

But that was only the beginning. As everyone knew, the scales of justice were depressed, and no student of late antique society can fail equally to be depressed, by the corrupt bias, bribery and ubiquitous influence-peddling discovered throughout the whole judicial system. As Cyprian said, "There is nothing to be afraid about in the laws. What is for sale is not feared"[10]--a good enough testimony to the character of litigation one might expect, though perhaps too breezily expressed. For after all, not everyone could pay the necessary price. Even a leading citizen might be repeatedly flogged, and so at last beaten to death, by the governor, for the crime of having no more wealth to reveal.[11] Poorer people could not always come up with the *douceurs*, "the little baskets, as we say," that were expected even in episcopal courts.[12] They certainly could not afford the price of buying office itself, generally expected within all branches of government, attested even inside the Church,[13] and recouped by the buyer through the collection of fees such as Dr. Chadwick mentions. So power, or we might call it justice, had a lot to do with money. But poor petitioners might get someone well placed to intercede on their behalf. For that, payment might be deferred, or never demanded. We see bishops putting in a good word for themselves or more often for humble dependents with all sorts of authorities, secular[14] or ecclesiastical.[15] Increasingly, bishops belonged to higher social strata,[16] being converts to a Church career from a governmental one, or senators, or *curiales* of large cities, or otherwise drawn from prominent and respected and therefore powerful backgrounds. They had all been to school together, and could appeal to a praetorian prefect as a boyhood chum.[17]

Appeal might not work. Though one would suppose, from reading the correspondence of notables of any period in the Empire, that everyone of the least influence was some-

---

[9]P. Garnsey, *Social Status and Legal Privilege* ... (1970).

[10]*Ad Donat.* 10, cf. generally my *Roman Government* ... (1976) 91f.; the eloquent preface to the fourth book of Firmicus Maternus' *Mathesis*; or A.H.M. Jones, *Later Roman Empire* (1964) 543-552.

[11]Synes., *Ep.* 72; or compare the death by flogging, for no convicted crime, in Liban., *Or.* 46.8, and others narrowly averted, *Or.* 1.170.

[12]As Dr. Chadwick points out: *Cod.Just.* 1.4.29.6, it was improper ἀμετρίᾳ τῶν καλουμένων σπορτούλων τοὺς ὑπομιμνησκομένους ἐπιτρίβειν, so (§7) the rates are set forth. I suppose the practice must have been established at least a couple of generations before the date of the law, AD 530.

[13]*Gesta apud Zenophilum*, cit., ed. Ziwsa p. 194.

[14]Dr. Chadwick instances Aug., *Ep.* 151-3; one could add endless illustration, for example, Greg. Naz., *Ep.* 9 and 21; Basil, *Ep.* 107, interesting because it explains some of the rules of procedure; and Synes., *Ep.* 17 and 44.

[15]Aug., *Ep.* 153.3.10 (*CSEL* XLIV p. 407), intercession with an angry bishop at Carthage.

[16]Most clearly seen in F.D. Gilliard, *Social Origins of Bishops in the Fourth Century*, Diss. California (Berkeley 1966) 60-62, 78, 80, 85, and passim.

[17]Appeal, but quite punctiliously, e.g. in Greg. Naz., *Ep.* 29 to Sophronius, praetorian prefect, childhood friend; Basil, *Ep.* 272.1.

how tied to everyone else by the exchange of letters of recommendation, producing the exchange of little favors, and that membership in this network constituted power itself, nevertheless, there were levels of difficulty not to be reached in this so-civilized manner. We are reminded of it, for example, by the efforts of the executive chief of the urban prefect's staff to secure the person of a material witness, a certain Felix. It is Fulgentius, a senator, who ends up with the man. "The chief of staff ran out with a retinue of a small number of men. He laid hold of Felix in a crowded part of the city, without getting him away. So Fulgentius, pretending he had been struck, resisted the law with a stronger body of men, while Felix was whisked off."[18] What wins are, just as Napoleon said, the bigger battalions, right in the broadest streets of Rome itself and against the decree of the courts and the subsequent complaints of the urban prefect. And we could easily multiply the instances of such things happening in the fourth and fifth centuries: the law is flouted, pure violence triumphs, and complaint is raised with or without success--it might be, by a bishop.[19]

In these centuries, how common are incidents of rough treatment and bodily harm! And those in which Church officials are involved actively or passively are not hard to find. A great deal of evidence clusters around the conflicts between those judged heretic and those who emerged as orthodox, perhaps the best known being the struggles in which Athanasius was involved.[20] But in Africa in 412, the emperor expressed the hope that "the admonitions of the landowners or often repeated thrashings would recall the peasants from a depraved worship," Donatism,[21] and Augustine expects the same, or almost the same, zeal in that good cause from the landowners that *he* addresses.[22] Given the vulnerability of the great mass of the empire's inhabitants, tenant farmers, rural laborers, and owners of a few acres in and out of debt, it is hardly surprising that we should see at work upon them the most fundamental and decisive kind of power, sheer brute force and economic advantage; nor is it surprising that Church leaders should be among those persons who exercise such power, through being the title-holders to various lands or whole villages or through being stationed among rural estates.[23]

When, therefore, we try to explain the power of bishops in the very most concrete and specific terms, as also the power of secular magnates not actually commanding troops, we should logically begin at the bottom, that is, with the exertion of the crudest force upon the humblest person: a *possessor* takes a stick to the back

---

[18]Symm., *Rel.* 23.11.

[19]E.g., Synes., *Ep.* 47.

[20]E.g., the story in H.I. Bell, *Jews and Christians* ... (1924) 60 (lines 46f., and passim).

[21]*Cod. Theod.* 16.5.52.4.

[22]*Ep.* 58, approving "the admonitions" of his correspondent to "your African peasants," and *Ep.* 66.1f., referring to the master of a *villa* or *fundus*, "whose peasants" have chosen sides in religion from *timor dominationis, coacti in falsitate.*

[23]Jerome, *Life of Malchus* 2, a bishop owns an entire village; *Gesta coll. Carth.* 181 (*PL* 11.1326), *in villis vel in fundis esse episcopos ordinatos*; Aug., *Ep.* 65.1, a presbyter *in fundo*; and abundant evidence of the Church owning great lists of *fundi*, from Constantine's donations onwards.

of his peasant, and so produces conversion. The scene can be made more complex *ad lib.* It is, let us suppose, not the estate owner but his bailiff, not the bailiff but some village toughs, not a few men but many, who terrorize. But at some needful point, the right man who knows the right man can engage his will in this machinery of altogether everyday compulsion.

At the furthest remove from such primitive kinds of power lies the word spoken by which the listener is persuaded not to speak, himself: he withholds a favor, a promotion, a loan, or the like. So insensible a thing as silence can be a form of power, that too brought to bear by someone speaking to the right man at the right point.

But with whatever crudeness or delicacy, with however direct or remote a connection to the persons made to obey, the power of ecclesiastical leaders thus far outlined exactly resembled that exercised by secular magnates. There was no difference at all.

Or rather, there was one difference. As Dr. Chadwick indicates, a bishop's "authority is grounded in his spirituality as an ascetic and holy man."[24] In all the ordinary, worldly ways he could make things happen: he controlled influence, money, suasion and knowledge of how and where decisions were arrived at. But beyond that, if he was crossed, your child might die, or you yourself fall ill, and recover only when you had repented (those were the tales told of Basil).[25] If we ask, then, what feeling animated those who heeded what he said, the answer must be fear, fear of the divine will that he could aim against the heedless. His like is hardly to be found before the mid-fourth century,[26] and Dr. Chadwick is surely correct in his final conclusion, that the Church introduced into the empire "a new type of leader" superadding, to the old, new types of power.

---

[24]Dr. Chadwick is here instancing Epiphanius; cf. his remarks later on Ambrose and the power to "preserve the favour of heaven."

[25]Soc., *H.E.* 4.26 ad fin.; Soz., *H.E.* 6.16; cf. Basil's later letters to Modestus the prefect, *Ep.* 104, 110f., etc.

[26]Pagan equivalents (we are not speaking of mere magicians now) are, to my knowledge, neither many nor close: Apollonius of Tyana, in such episodes as those at Aspendus and Ephesus, Philostr., *Vit.Apollon.* 1.15 and 7.7.8f., and Eustathius, in Eunap., *Vit.soph.* 466. For Christian holy men and their power, see the very interesting first section of P. Brown's essay, *Jnl.Rom.Stud.* 61 (1971) 81f.

Response by Dr. Massey H. Shepherd, Jr.
Professor of Liturgics, Graduate Theological Union, Berkeley

Professor Chadwick's paper covers, with his customary acumen, all of the Christian bishop's roles in antiquity, both those that were internal in the Church, and those that were external in relation to society. In this response I shall confine myself to certain supplementary notes, all of which are certainly well-known to Professor Chadwick; but they may provide further background for the discussion of our colloquy. I shall confine myself in the main, though not entirely, to the pre-Constantinian period.

1. Monoepiscopacy. The monarchical episcopate first comes clearly into view in the letters of Ignatius of Antioch to churches in Asia Minor. I would date them *ca.* 115.[1] It is clear from these letters that the bishop's sole authority, in matters of doctrine and worship, was not yet firmly established among all who claimed to be Christians in this area.[2] Whether the office of bishop was originally distinct from that of the presbyter, or a particular function of ministry appointed to one of the presbyters, remains a matter of long-standing dispute which we need not discuss here. Other documents of approximately Ignatius' date--1 Clement and the Pastoral Epistles--show a certain ambiguity about the distinction between bishops and presbyters, the latter being a collegial body comparable to the presbyters of Jewish communities.[3]

In the larger cities, where there were more than one congregation or house-church, there might have been a bishop for each congregation--again, comparable to the ruler of a synagogue in Jewish communities. The emergence of a single bishop in each city was due in part, as Professor Chadwick indicates (p. 3), to "the conflict with heresy" that threatened the preservation of apostolic teaching. The bishop was in a favorable position to become "the personal focus of ecclesial unity" because he was both the presiding minister of the Eucharist, and from its offerings, with the help of his deacons, the dispenser of charity. He would thus decide who would be allowed, if not himself, to preach and teach at the church assemblies, and who would be eligible for church aid. No one was to do anything pertaining to the church, according to Ignatius, except on authority of the bishop or of one whom he appointed as his deputy.[4]

As Professor Chadwick pointed out (p. 5), the bishop had a special *charisma* for his office by virtue of his ordination.[5] This was long challenged, however, by "prophets and teachers" who claimed a higher *charisma* which was not conferred by human mediaries. In the time of the Pastorals and Ignatius and Polycarp, these were the Docetists and Gnostics. In answer to them, Ignatius said that he had prophesied in the Spirit with "the voice of God" (*Phil.* 7; cf. *Poly.* 2:2). Later, Polycarp's church in Smyrna called him "an apostolic and prophetic teacher and bishop" (*Mart. Poly.* 16:2).

---

[1]See G. Downey, *A History of Antioch in Syria* (1961) 292-293.

[2]Cf. *Smyr.* 8, *Poly.* 3-4, and probably *Eph.* 5.

[3]See commentary of M. Dibelius and H. Conzelmann, *The Pastoral Epistles*, ed. by H. Koester, *Hermeneia* series (1972) 50-59, 77-79, 132-134.

[4]*Smyr.* 8; see my article, "Smyrna in the Ignatian Letters: A Study in Church Order," *The Journal of Religion* 20 (1940) 141-159.

[5]1 Tim. 4:14, 2 Tim. 1:6; cf. the ordination prayer in Hippolytus, *Apostolic Tradition* 3.

In the latter part of the second century, the challenge came from the "New Prophecy" of the Montanists. Out of this conflict came the first references to synods of bishops, in which the disturbers of the peace were excommunicated, not so much for heresy as for insubordination (Eusebius, *H.E.* v.16, 10 and 19, 1-4). In the third century, attacks on the bishops by charismatics centered in the question of discipline of moral offenders. Tertullian, as Montanist, excoriated the Bishop of Carthage for his policy of penance for sexual sins (*De pudicitia* 1); and Hippolytus at Rome similarly castigated Bishop Callistus for a similar regulation, and also for the bishop's "monarchianism" (*Refutatio omnium haeresium* x.2). Hippolytus formed his own church, considering himself a bishop able to communicate whatever the Spirit should provide in his teaching.[6] The final struggle came in the Decian persecution of 250-251, when the martyrs and confessors, by virtue of their extraordinary *charisma*, usurped the bishop's right to be the sole arbiter of penance and absolution for "the lapsed" (Cyprian, *De lapsis* and many letters). Out of this conflict came the schism of Novatian.

2. Persecution. Another important factor in the unification of the local church around a single bishop was the external pressure of persecution. Although Nero's attack on Christians in Rome in July 64 provided a precedent, the rescript of Trajan in 112, moderate as it was, gave the first clear legal basis.[7] Although most of the martyrs in the second and third centuries were not bishops, there is some indication that the martyrdom of a bishop could be crucial for the defection or intensified devotion of his flock. Ignatius left a divided flock in Syria, as attested in all his letters. The martyrdom of Bishop Publius of Athens (probably about the same time) left his flock "all but apostatized from the Word" (Dionysius of Corinth in Eusebius *H.E.* iv.23.2). On the other hand, Polycarp's witness at Smyrna and Bishop Pothinus' suffering at Lyons seems to have strengthened their churches' loyalty to the faith.

By the middle of the third century, Christians had become sufficiently numerous so that empire-wide persecutions replaced the earlier local attempts to contain them. In Decius' persecution bishops of more eminent sees were often the first victims. Bishop Fabian of Rome was the first to suffer, and was soon followed by Bishops Babylas of Antioch and Alexander of Jerusalem. Bishops Dionysius of Alexandria and Cyprian of Carthage managed to escape into hiding. It was more than a year before the Roman church was able to elect a new bishop; for, as Cyprian reported, Decius had said that he feared a new bishop in Rome more than a rival to his throne (*Epist.* lv.9,1). Valerian's first edict in 257 led to the arrest of Cyprian and Dionysius. Cyprian was executed a year later; Dionysius, banished to Libya, managed to survive. But the edict of 258, under which Cyprian was martyred, also saw the slaughter of Bishop Xystus II of Rome and his deacons and the immolation of Bishop Fructuosus of Tarragona and his deacons.

3. Election and Ordination. The selection of a bishop in the early Church is not always very clear as to the procedures. Professor Chadwick (p. 1) states that "his authority is acknowledged in the consent of the plebs to his consecration," but he then cites Hippolytus (*Apostolic Tradition* 2) that the bishop is elected by all the people.

---

[6]*Ibid.*, i. proem. The author of the *Refutatio* was certainly an antagonist in Rome of Bishop Callistus. But the challenge of P. Nautin to the modern reconstruction of the career and writings of Hippolytus in his *Hippolyte et Josipe* (1947) and his other works on this subject, do not seem to me to have been successfully answered. For another critique, based on archaeological evidence, see A. Amore, "Note su S. Ippolito Martire," *Rivista di archeologia cristiana* 30 (1954) 63-97.

[7]See J. Moreau, *La persécution du christianisme dans l'empire romain* (1956) 40-46.

Granted the difficulties of a secure text (from the many versions and expansions of the original), the rubrics of the text suggest that the new bishop's election by "all the people" is, in fact, a nomination that is acceptable. On the appointed Sunday when the people assemble with the presbyters and visiting bishops, the consent of all is again requested before the ordination by the bishops alone begins. It is not clear whether the presbyters participated in the nomination-election; but the Greek version in the *Apostolic Constitutions* viii.4 (ed. F.X. Funk, p. 472) includes them in this preliminary choice. Another obscurity is the phrase *consentientibus omnibus*, immediately before the ordination. Does the "all consenting" include everyone present, or only the presbyters and bishops, or simply the bishops? (H.B. Porter, Jr., *The Ordination Prayers of the Ancient Western Churches* [ACC XLIX] [1967] 7, interprets it as referring only to the bishops.)

The evidence from Cyprian's letters about the election and ordination of Bishop Cornelius at Rome (*Epist.* lv.8) and of the Bishops of Leon and Merida in Spain (*Epist.* lxvii.4-5), to replace two bishops who had lapsed in the persecution, is basically in accord with Hippolytus. Cyprian, however, speaks of only one assembly when the new bishop was chosen by the people and clergy and the neighboring bishops of the province. The bishops only lay on hands in ordination. Eusebius relates the circumstances of the election and ordination of Bishops Alexander of Jerusalem[8] and Fabian of Rome (*H.E.* vi.10-11, and 29). These accord with the evidence from Cyprian, except that Eusebius was especially interested in supernatural signs that indicated to the people God's choice of their bishop.

Cyprian stated that this method of selection and ordination prevailed in "almost all the provinces" (*Epist.* lxvii.5). He does not name the exceptions; but one of them was probably Egypt. Controversy about episcopal succession in Alexandria still goes on.[9] My own opinion is that the bishops of Alexandria down to 328 were elected by the twelve presbyters of the city from among their number and were ordained by them. Athanasius, while still a deacon, was the first to be chosen and ordained in the customary way--perhaps as a result of the fourth canon of Nicaea, 325.[10]

Changes in the process of appointment of bishops that followed the Constantinian peace need a new and thorough assessment. This would involve a study of the increasing role of the metropolitan--and, indeed, of the emperor--in the choice of candidates and how this choice was exercized; the diminution of the laity's rights in their selection, and even in certain circumstances of their assent; the problem of nepotism; the use of constraint on unwilling bishops-elect; conciliar interventions; the practice of schismatic churches such as the Novatians and the Donatists; and so forth.

---

[8]Alexander is the first instance known of a bishop translated from one see to another, and of occupying his second see while his predecessor Narcissus was still alive. Actually, Narcissus was very old--we would say today that he "retired"--but he continued to share the honor of the episcopate with Alexander. According to Eusebius, the translation of Alexander was due to a divine revelation imparted to him and to the people of Jerusalem.

[9]W. Telfer, "Episcopal Succession in Egypt," *The Journal of Ecclesiastical History* 3 (1957) 1-13. This was answered by E.W. Kemp, "Bishops and Presbyters at Alexandria," *Ibid.* 6 (1955) 125-142. E. Ferguson, "Origen and the Election of Bishops," *Church History* 43 (1974) 26-33, agrees, in general, with Telfer.

[10]Athanasius' election may not have been unanimous. He himself admitted that it was by a "majority": *Apologia contra Arianos* 6. Arian calumnies about it are recorded in Sozomen, *H.E.* ii.17; Philostorgius, *H.E.* ii.11.

4. Social status. The early Christians before the time of Constantine, since their religion was illicit, were not interested in the social origins or status of their bishops before their conversion. In any case, we know almost nothing about the matter. J.B. Lightfoot's conjecture that Clement, the third bishop of Rome, was "a freedman or the son of a freedman belonging to the household of Flavius Clemens," a cousin of the emperor Domitian,[11] is possible but not provable. We know from Hippolytus that Bishop Victor had access to, and obtained favors from, a Christian concubine of the emperor Commodus named Marcia, whose foster-father was one of his presbyters (*Refutatio* ix.12).[12]

By the middle of the third century, when Christianity had become more numerous, we begin to glean names of bishops from either noble or wealthy families. Among the earliest that are known were two brothers from an aristocratic family of Pontus, Theodore (better known as Gregory) and Athenodore. On their way to study law in Berytus, they stopped in Caesarea, where they came under the spell of Origen; after five years under his tutelage, they returned to their native land and soon were made missionary bishops (Eusebius, *H.E.* vi.30). Gregory, whose see was Neo-Caesarea, became known as the "Wonder-Worker" (*Thaumaturgus*); and a century later, Gregory of Nyssa said of him, in a panegyric, not always reliable, that he had found only seventeen Christians there, but when he died (*ca.* 270) there were only seventeen pagans!

Perhaps the wealthiest of the pre-Constantinian bishops was Cyprian of Carthage, who became bishop in 249 not long after his conversion. His career is too well-known to be recounted here. Despite his efforts after his conversion to conceal everything about his pagan past, it is probable that some of his former friends assisted in providing his safe refuge, where he could see visitors and carry on his correspondence during the Decian persecution. When he was arrested in the Valerian persecution, he was given unusual consideration and, in fact, an opportunity for flight. Banished for a time to Curubis, he was later allowed to live under house arrest in his own home and gardens in Carthage. At his execution on September 14, 258, his flock was allowed, without hindrance, to attend his martyrdom and to give him a public funeral.

In the liturgical calendar of the West, Cyprian is associated with his colleague at Rome, Bishop Cornelius (251-253). Cornelius had neither the status nor the education of Cyprian; but he bore the name of an aristocratic Roman family. The emperor Gallus banished him to Circumcellae (Civitavecchia), where he died. There is no evidence that he was subjected to hard labor. His body, brought back to Rome, was buried in a crypt in a *praedium* belonging to the family of the Caecilii, and not in the church's catacomb nearby (that of Callistus), where there was a special crypt for the third-century popes. Access to this tomb was not available to the faithful before the latter part of the fourth century. It is interesting that when his tomb was found in modern times the inscription on it was in Latin, whereas the inscriptions on the tombs of the popes in the papal crypt in Callistus were all in Greek letters, whether their names were Greek or Latin. It may well be that Cornelius was a member or a client of the household of the wealthy family that gave him his private burial.[13]

---

[11]*The Apostolic Fathers*, Part I, S. Clement of Rome [1890], I, 1, p. 61.

[12]An affluent layman in Rome in Victor's time and a member of Caesar's household (probably a freedman of Marcus Aurelius; cf. *C.I.L.* vi.13040), by the name of Carpophorus, was the master of the slave Callistus, who would become the second successor after Victor as Bishop of Rome.

[13]See my article, "The Liturgical Reform of Damasus I," *Kyriakon, Festschrift Johannes Quasten*, ed. by P. Granfield and J.A. Jungmann (1970) II. 852-853 and 861-863.

Dionysius "the Great," Bishop of Alexandria, 247-264, had been a man of wealth and "worldly dignity" (Eusebius, *H.E.* vii.11,18). Like his predecessor, Bishop Heraclas, 233-247, he had been a convert from paganism and had become a pupil of Origen, and was perhaps the most distinguished Christian theologian and philosopher of his time among the bishops. He, too, like Cyprian, had been exiled in the Valerian persecution rather than summarily executed; but unlike Cyprian, he managed to survive. Another distinguished bishop, who had studied with Origen, was Firmilian of Caesarea in Cappadocia, *ca.* 230-268.[14] It was he who rallied the "Origenist" bishops of the East to seek the unseating of Paul of Samosata, Bishop of Antioch, 260-268.

Paul's story is an interesting one. It is told, with considerable venom, in the encyclical letter of the bishops who deposed and excommunicated him in 268 (Eusebius, *H.E.* vii.30). Of a poor family, he made himself rich in the practice of law. During the Palmyrene control of Syria under King Odenathus and his Queen Zenobia, he was made, during his episcopate, a *ducenarius*, i.e., a financial official charged with the collection of taxes, in which office he seems to have behaved in a high-handed manner.[15] Because of Zenobia's favor, the bishops were unable to dislodge Paul from his cathedral until the emperor Aurelian defeated and captured the queen in 272.[16] Petition was then made to the emperor to remove Paul, which he did after receiving a written communication from the bishops of Italy and Rome (Eusebius, *H.E.* vii.30,19). The decision of Aurelian, who was certainly no friend of Christianity, was not in any way related to ecclesiastical issues, but was purely a matter of deciding a legal case of property ownership based on Gallienus' restoration of 260.[17]

Other bishops in the latter half of the third century rose to prominence not only in their churches but in the larger world of learning. Eusebius mentions a few (*H.E.* vii.32). One of these, Anatolius, a native of Alexandria, was so erudite in many fields of rhetoric, science, and philosophy, that his fellow-citizens had him establish a school of the Aristotelian tradition. Later he became Bishop of Laodicea in Syria. Another, Bishop Meletius of Sebastopolis in Pontus, was accomplished in literature, and was of such eloquence that his name was used for a nickname: the "honey of Attica." For seven years he was a refugee in the persecution of Diocletian, but lived to attend the Council of Nicaea in 325 (Philostorgius, *H.E.* i.8). When one adds to these the names of many learned presbyters of this period, mentioned by Eusebius, the Church was not totally unprepared for the new roles of public leadership that were thrust upon it by Constantine.

---

[14]L. Duchesne, *Early History of the Christian Church* I (1909) 318, spoke of him as "a man of high birth;" but I cannot find the source of this, unless it be Eusebius (*H.E.* vi.27), who called him "eminent" (διαπρεπής).

[15]The bishops' letter accused him of extortion and fraud; but this may be a calumny. In *De lapsis* 6, Cyprian complained of bishops who took secular jobs, who were greedy for money and practiced fraud and usury. Since he gave no particular instances, however, he may have been exercising some rhetorical exaggeration.

[16]The bishops' letter does not mention Zenobia, perhaps for politic reasons, since their synod of 268 was held in Antioch. Athanasius, *Hist. Arian.* 71, was the first to record Paul's support by her. The church building, where Paul had set up his throne, and which he refused to hand over upon his deposition, was probably the first cathedral of a Christian bishop. It was destroyed in the Diocletian persecution (Theodoret, *H.E.* i.2).

[17]Eusebius, *H.E.* vii.13; Downey, *op.cit.* 315, for a contrary view.

MINUTES OF THE COLLOQUY OF 25 FEBRUARY 1979

List of Participants

Professor at *Oxford University, England*
Henry Chadwick *(Dean of Christ Church)*

Professors at the *University of California, Berkeley*
William S. Anderson *(Latin and Comparative Literature)*
Julian C. Boyd *(English)*
Peter Brown *(Classics and History)*
Gerard Caspary *(History)*
John Dillon *(Classics)*
John Kenney *(Associate Specialist, Law)*
Anitra Bingham Kolenkow *(Lecturer, Religious Studies)*
Charles E. Murgia *(Classics)*
Wayne Shumaker *(English, Emeritus)*
Tu Wei-ming *(History)*
David H. Wright *(History of Art)*

Professors at the *Graduate Theological Union*
John L. Bogart *(Continuing Education)*
Michael J. Buckley *(Systematic Theology)*
Michael L. Cook *(Systematic Theology)*
Mary Ann Donovan *(Historical Theology)*
Victor R. Gold *(Old Testament)*
Edward C. Hobbs *(Theology and Hermeneutics)*
Sherman E. Johnson *(New Testament; and Dean, CDSP, Emeritus)*
Thomas W. Leahy *(Biblical Studies)*
John Hilary Martin *(Historical Theology)*
Ted F. Peters *(Systematic Theology)*
Massey H. Shepherd, Jr. *(Liturgics)*
Herman C. Waetjen *(New Testament)*
Kevin Wall *(Theology and Philosophy)*
Claude Welch *(Historical Theology; and Dean, GTU)*
David Winston *(Hellenistic and Judaic Studies)*
John H. Wright *(Systematic Theology)*
Wilhelm Wuellner *(New Testament)*
Marvin Brown *(Visiting Scholar)*

Professors at *Pacific Union College*
Eric D. Syme *(History)*
Fred Veltman *(Religion)*

Professor at the *University of Calgary, Alberta, Canada*
David H. Stewart *(Anthropology)*

Professor at the *University of California, San Francisco Medical Center*
Otto E. Guttentag *(Medical Philosophy, Emeritus)*

Professor at the *University of San Francisco*
John H. Elliott *(Exegetical Theology)*

Professor at the *University of Texas*
Daniel Matt *(Medieval Hebrew Literature)*

Students
John Engeln, Irene Lawrence *(Recording Secretary)*, Daniel Rothwell,
Daryl Schmidt (*GTU*) Carole Straw (*UCB*)

MINUTES OF THE COLLOQUY OF 25 FEBRUARY 1979

THE DISCUSSION

Summarized by Irene Lawrence

Chadwick: I would like to thank my critics very much for their kindness and for the illumination that their comments throw on a complicated problem, although I could not agree with one or two things Professor MacMullen has said. Rereading my text I have become conscious of some omissions, I hope unimportant.

I certainly ought to have said something about bishops as the means by which the feminine voice was likely to become articulated, as Professor Brown points out, and also about the emancipation of slaves. That was more important in the earlier period, and I should like to know of evidence that after Constantine bishops went on emancipating slaves on any large scale. My impression is that they did not.

We might want to discuss anti-clericalism, which is more or less coeval and coterminous with Christianity. My paper is almost silent about it.

I ought to have said something about the rule against translations from one see to another. They did occur, but they were unusual. The rule made for long tenure. At least one bishop, Proculus of Marseilles in the late fourth and early fifth centuries, held his see for over fifty years.

The story I wanted to put before you is the story of how the bishop came to have his position within the community of the Spirit; his authority was certainly dependent on his personal holiness and the worthiness of his life, but it was also dependent on his proper succession. He had the *cura* of souls in his church; a metropolitan had the *cura* of many churches; a patriarch or the Bishop of Rome had the *cura* of an enormous number of churches. That could be justified by the power of the keys. The bishop was always liable to be questioned by various charismatic characters, but most of them acknowledged that the bishop too had some charismatic power. There is the story of the two Gaza hesychasts at the time of Justinian, Barsanuphius and John. Someone asked Barsanuphius who had the power of the keys, and he answered, "There is the Bishop of Rome, whose name is John [II], there is Elias of Corinth"--of whom we otherwise know nothing--"and there is a holy man in the region of Gaza"--himself.

The shepherd of souls will be answerable at the Last Judgement for the way his flock has behaved, and that was the ultimate locus of his authority. He had authority because his flock wanted him to have it; it was not an autocracy imposed from without.

The bishop became part of the "Establishment"; we have the paradox of an ex-slave (Callistus) becoming Bishop of Rome only a few years before the first known episcopal senator, Cyprian, became Bishop of Carthage. Cyprian was certainly well-connected, as is demonstrated by that extraordinary letter which shows that he received intelligence of the imperial decree announcing the persecution of the church some weeks before the proconsul of

North Africa knew about it. In other words, there was somebody at court whom we may call "Deep Throat."

I am conscious of two other omissions in my paper. One is the accessibility of bishops. We have testimony in the *Confessions* of Augustine about the complete accessibility of Ambrose, although Augustine was too shy to speak to him. Did he just sit in the cathedral at Milan and let anyone come and talk to him? The other gap is that I did not say enough about the bishop in later times as an interceder for military victory. The role of Bishop Valens at the Battle of Mursa in 351 is well attested. The most dramatic account is in the Mozarabic *Liber Ordinum*, which records in meticulous detail the rites and ceremonies in the cathedral at Toledo when the Visigothic king goes forth to war.

This story is about how the successor of God's fishermen found himself becoming a member of the Establishment. He did not always like it, and he was always liable to be reminded that his education and social background were actually not the reasons why he had authority within the community.

Wuellner: All of the responses (pp. 15-34) center around various aspects of alternative forms of authority practiced in Late Antiquity. That might suggest the focus for our discussion tonight.

Dillon: Would you comment on situations like Demetrius of Alexandria vis-à-vis Origen? Bishops seem to face problems from independent theologians of dangerous views--like Hans Küng.

Gold: First, would the delineation between the city bishop and the country bishop fit into the later expansion of Islam? That is frequently attributed to the neglect of the country dioceses, since Islam swung around many urban areas and occupied the rural districts. Second, there was a change in the way bishops were elected, especially in the East; they began to be selected from the monastic orders. It was assumed that others had interests other than piety. Third, the beginnings of episcopal power lay originally in the non-political. But as the political power in the West began to deteriorate, it was natural, although perhaps unconscious, for the bishop to take the place of the Roman administrators.

P. Brown: I would like to raise the problem of pro-clericalism--the way in which the bishop's authority soon came, even for groups beyond the church, to sum up an ideal type of authority. When Ambrose was appointed governor of Emilia, Petronius Probus, who as an administrator was not himself entirely clean-handed, said, "Go and govern *as if you were a bishop*."

One problem about the relation between the bishops and the monastic movement was that the great monastic leaders were taking over, in the different environment of the monasteries, the image of the bishop--of the all-seeing, authoritative, mild father. Urban conditions of the third and fourth centuries made it increasingly hard for the bishop to live up to that image; the abbott could.

Shepherd: We have tended to approach the subject of the bishop's authority topically, but there are important differences geographically. The Bishop of Alexandria was the "Pope of popes" in the early church. Despite the claims of the Roman see, the North Africans were willing to accept Rome's authority when it agreed with them doctrinally, but they were not in the least prepared to accept Rome's intervention in jurisdiction. In a more chaotic area like Gaul, there were problems of papal authority over the bishops of Arles: Patroclus and Hilary. The metropolitan structure varies considerably. Antioch, for example, the largest in extent, seems to have been the weakest in external authority, losing Constantinople, then Jerusalem, then Cyprus.

Caspary: Several questions are raised: How early did the social class that the bishops belonged to begin to climb? What role did laymen, women, and the poor really play? When and to what extent did the care of the poor in the country become part of the *cura* of the bishop?

Kolenkow: There is the question of the bishop's negative power--what he might do to someone who opposed him (MacMullen) compared to his positive power--what he can do as a rhetor and intercessor.

Schmidt: Some of these issues remind me of the way Walter Bauer put the issue for the second century (in *Orthodoxy and Heresy in Earliest Christianity*) about local communities engaged in an open-ended struggle to determine what in fact would become orthodoxy. Hindsight tends to follow the stream that was later regarded as orthodox.

[Here D. Wright presented a series of slides illustrating the public image projected by the bishop as a patron of public art. Beginning with the fourth century inscription of Theodore, Bishop of Aquileia (mentioned by Professor Chadwick, p. 13), D. Wright illustrated how the growing importance of the founding bishop was represented by more prominent inscriptions, then by pictorial representations, first in a subordinate position, and eventually on the same level as the patron saint in mid-seventh-century Greece. The Latin church, however, continued to represent founding bishops in such a way as to maintain a suitable distance between the bishop and the patron saint. By implication, this represented the ground of the bishop's authority.]

Buckley: On p. 10, you cite as an axiom "That the right form of worship is essential if heaven is to be propitious," to which Christians added the belief that right worship presupposed right doctrine; and that explains pagan persecutions of Christians and the ferocity of Christian sectarian conflicts. Can that be substantiated? The concern for "right doctrine" appears in earliest Christianity, in the Johannine epistles and in Galatians, for example.

Wall: On p. 3, it says, "The conflict with heresy made it a practical necessity to make one presiding figure the personal focus of ecclesial unity in the local congregation." I take that to mean that the faith must be one, and it cannot be one without one presiding figure. Again, on p. 5, the description of authority as "from the bottom upwards" seems to mean, not from the lower classes, but from the local community, which is convinced there must be unity of faith, and there will not be, unless there is one bishop.

<u>Chadwick</u>: I would like to start with the issue of "theologians of dangerous views." I suspect that at all times bishops regard all theologians of very high ability as persons who could be so described. In the case of Demetrius and Origen, there were some personal factors, and Origen in any case was very hostile to bishops, as shown in his commentary on Matthew 23. "Woe to you who, although scribes and pharisees, are hypocrites." Bishops seem to him the most striking living exemplars of the faults which are there excoriated. What should one expect of a man who comments on bishops' ordination with these words: "You would almost think that the prime purpose of this ceremony was to give these men the opportunity for the public renunciation of humility." Origen is passionately ascetic, so merciless and relentless, that one admires him, but thanks heaven that he is not to be in charge at the Last Judgement.

We are unfortunately very little informed about whether the church conquered the country or not. There is the familiar facetiousness of Orosius about the fact that in his time (415) the country folk were *pagani*. Islam certainly did sweep the countryside with extraordinary rapidity, but it may not be all Christian neglect; it may be partly the deep-rooted conservatism and paganism of the countryside. Had there been a fourth-century Harvey Cox, he would have written a book on the secular countryside. Yet we know of some cities that were Christian to a man in the time of Constantine.

It is true that as the Western imperial administration began to decline the authority of the bishops increased. And many persons like Sidonius Apollinaris of Clermont found the bishop's office the most useful way of serving society, and not just spiritually.

Regarding pro-clericalism, some bishops were very popular. To get Liberius out of Rome, Constantius had to arrange to have him kidnapped in the middle of the night, or there would have been a riot. We also know of a number of unpopular bishops; people tended to think that bishops--with some individual exceptions--were on their side. Theophilus of Alexandria was one of the most ambivalent. Synesius seems to think he was rather good, but Palladius's Life of Chrysostom takes a different view.

There were great regional divergences; no ancient patriarch, not even the Bishop of Rome, exercised as much autocracy as the ancient bishops of Alexandria. People argued with the bishops of Rome, especially if they were so imprudent as to give reasons. The papacy got involved in taking sides in an internal Gallic row between Arles and Vienne. And poor Antioch was weakened partly because at the critical stage in the fourth century it was so racked by schism that there seemed to be always at least two bishops, and at one stage four.

The Ignatian desire to concentrate Eucharistic communion on the personal authority of one man was related to unity in faith; they did seem to think that the unity needed a focus. But the monarchical bishop was not unutterably transcendent in relation to his presbyters; he addressed them as "my fellow presbyters," and he shared the *sacerdotium* with them.

My principal disagreement with Professor MacMullen was that, although he gives a marvelous series of acute comments, he seemed to me writing in the light of modern university experience, as if ancient riots were caused by the students or their equivalent not being consulted. Yet the evidence for people in antiquity having riots whether or not they were consulted seems to me quite considerable.

I also very much doubt whether people can be simply beaten into church, unless they feel that is where they really ought to be. The famous Hawker of Morwenstow in Cornwall could whip his parishioners into church, but only because his parishioners agreed with him.

Shepherd: A footnote about Origen: he owed his position in Alexandria to Demetrius appointing him, while still quite young, to head the catechetical school which Demetrius had opened after a brief persecution. The grounds of Demetrius's excommunication of Origen were canonical, not theological. Of course, a personal antipathy may have led him to find a canonical excuse. Origen was highly regarded by the bishops in Palestine who ordained him; so Origen's tirades about bishops may be rooted in the fact that for Origen, authority comes primarily not through one's office, but through the spiritual endowment of the Word. In this sense, he was the father of the ascetics. He was a lay person during his early Alexandrian period, and even in Caesarea he was primarily a preacher.

The West, generally speaking, had less trouble with theologians than the East, because so many Eastern churches elected theologians to the episcopate. Hence the terrible theological rows. The Roman church, more often than not, elected a deacon or archdeacon--the administrator, particularly of charity--who were not especially interested in theological discussion. The dogmatic decisions of the Bishops of Rome stick closely to a canonical tradition of orthodoxy; they do not speculate.

P. Brown: We have not yet mentioned the conversion of Constantine. One of the interesting new looks on the early church is that, in some ways, it was not very important. Yet since we are dealing not only with the authority of the bishop, but also with his role in society, we should ask about his relations with the laity, and particularly with the lay patron. As emperor, Constantine's position as lay patron was overpowering; he could outbid any other lay patron. It would be interesting to imagine what would have happened if the emperor had not become Christian and so left the church to the patronage of local laymen and laywomen. In the Nestorian churches of Persia, and later under Islam, there is a totally different relation between lay patron and clergy. Perhaps one of the advantages of early Germanic Arianism was that, by not being Catholic, the German rulers and courtiers could not intervene in the affairs of the Catholic church. The overmighty local patron was a problem which Constantine solved for the church by outbidding any rivals.

Kolenkow: What about the bishop's and the emperor's range of power? It was said that the emperor was the one figure who had a double type of power like the bishop, both spiritual and political.

Caspary: More needs to be said about the enormous negative power of bishops in the late fourth century. Someone like Ambrose has tremendous power, even over the emperor, but it is of a very different type from the power of the emperor with his armies.

<u>Shepherd</u>: Ambrose is different from most bishops. He belonged to the highest Roman aristocracy, and thus was a formidable figure, bishop or not. He dealt with Arian and Orthodox rulers differently. As a priest, he had impact on the devout and orthodox Theodosius. But to the Arian dowager empress, although he showed spiritual courage, he did not have the same authority. Other bishops, with different social backgrounds, such as Chrysostom, were not so effective.

<u>Dillon</u>: The rules for electing successors are described on pp. 3-4. In one example, Anatolius (who may be the teacher of Iamblichus and a friend of Porphyry) was almost made Bishop of Caesarea by Theotecnus personally. But he was called away, and nabbed on his way back by the Laodiceans, and made Bishop of Laodicea, presumably a more democratic procedure. How often did a bishop succeed in appointing his successor and getting it to stick?

<u>Chadwick</u>: Bishops did try to appoint their successors when they saw a likely lad, partly to try to avert a riot. Leontius, Bishop of Antioch, used to point to his white hair and say, "When this snow melts, there will be much mud." And he was right. There was.

It was always dangerous for a bishop without a see to be traveling; someone might get hold of him. Proclus was ordained to Cyzicus in the fifth century, but they would not have him. So he spent his time in Constantinople until the see eventually became available to him. This was the reverse of the coin: he was consecrated by the Patriarch, but the local community would not accept him.

<u>Dillon</u>: The quorum of "two or three" was for the fourth century, but it sounds as if the norm was not clear earlier.

<u>Chadwick</u>: The evidence of Novatian's three consecrators suggests that three was the norm. Cornelius is very rude about the three consecrators and questions their sobriety, but not their sufficiency. Novatian was asking for trouble, and had there been anything wrong, Cornelius would not have failed to tell us. There were intolerable situations when three bishops consecrated someone in defiance of their colleagues, and this was a strong element in the origins of the Donatists.

<u>J. Wright</u>: On p. 32, Professor Shepherd says that in his opinion "the bishops of Alexandria down to 328 were elected by the twelve presbyters of the city from among their number and were ordained by them." Does this mean that no other bishops were involved in the consecration?

<u>Shepherd</u>: The method of consecration is much debated; I am not ready to go quite as far as Dr. Telfer's macabre idea that when the Bishop of Alexandria died, he was placed on his throne, and the twelve presbyters had the dead bishop lay his hand on the successor--although anything is possible in Alexandria. I do not know of any evidence before Athanasius that anyone except the presbyters were involved in the election. Origen and others witness that it was generally thought too riotous to have all the people involved. Part of the confusion is due to the ambiguity of "bishop" and "presbyter" in some traditions of the early church. Irenaeus calls bishops "presbyters." The question for the early church is more of succession to an accepted office than the manner by which one is put in it.

Gold: I was interested in the bishop's concern for the poor and the status of women. The church has recently been accused of two things. One, that its concern for the poor remains nominal, not a lived concern. Two, its concern for the disenfranchised, particularly women, has not always been evident. To understate this, it is rare that a woman has become bishop or pope in the Western church, bur poor people have.

Leahy: What evidence is there, and at what period, that bishops in antiquity accepted the claims of the bishops of Rome to be successors, not only of the apostles, but specifically of Peter, chief of the apostles? To what extent did the other bishops accept the Bishop of Rome's leadership role, based on the Petrine succession?

Dillon: It seems rather rare that a totally illegal alternative life style and system of justice and social welfare becomes legal, as the ecclesiastical courts did under Constantine and his successors. Compare modern organizations like the Sicilian Mafia, which almost becomes a law in Sicily. But the legal authorities and the Mafia show no willingness to integrate their systems.

Martin: The paper describes various functional types of episcopal authority, and it was pointed out that the bishops had this authority because the people wanted them to. What is the ideology of the reasons the people wanted it? What reasons were offered?

Shepherd: There are two reasons why Constantine gave legal authority to the bishops. One, the bishops already had some experience in settling internal disputes, going back to Paul's admonition about not going before secular judges. So there was already a structure in the church. Second, appointing new civil judges would only add to the existing corruption. Using the bishops meant less corruption and swifter justice.

Dillon: On the same grounds, it might not be a bad idea to hand over large sections of the inner city to the Black Panthers, and parts of Belfast to the IRA.

P. Brown: Professor Chadwick shows evidence that people really expected charisma from the bishop as arbitrator. He was thought to search souls and thus to know more about a situation than ordinary men. People in the third century expected more from the Christian bishop in that direction than we often allow for.

Wuellner: That seems to change within a century.*

---

*"The first monastic leaders (i.e. Anthony and Pachomius) completed an evolution begun by the bishops of the third century. Groups formed by a crisis of human relations (such as the 'increasingly unmanageable Christian communities of the third century') needed to invest their leaders with a supernatural ability to handle these" (so P. Brown, *The Making of Late Antiquity* 1978, p. 95 and n. 59 on p. 128 with reference to J. H. Waszink's collection of "evidence of the considerable role of the καρδιογνώστης in Early Christian communities").

Chadwick: The bishop is understood to be a charismatic character from the start, as the pastoral epistles show. Ordination was not just an investiture with rulebook and rod; it was also the bestowal of a charism of the spirit, concerned with the discernment of truth, and naturally extended to the bishop's court, where truth is often the issue at stake.

The ground of authority was of course partly that the people wanted it, but there are graver reasons. The bishop was the normal celebrant at the Eucharist and probably preached often, although it is curiously difficult to find out just how often he preached. Those who consecrated him were representatives of the *catholica*, and therefore linked him to the universal church, which he then represented to his congregation. That was an important ground of his authority to his congregation, just as his congregation was the ground of his authority to the *catholica*.

Problems of hospitality were considerable. Cyprian's correspondence shows the difficulties. When there were two bishops of Carthage and two bishops of Rome, and delegations were exchanged, accepting hospitality from the wrong faction was a very grave matter.

P. Brown: It is the universalism of the Christian institutions which is a new element. It is easy to find partial analogs, but a local power exercised on behalf of a universal group needs explaining.

Chadwick: There is no parallel to it in other societies. The closest are the "ecumenical synods" of actors and athletes.

I think the ancient church took it for granted that the see of Peter and Paul was a church of great authority and leadership. Problems began to arise toward the end of the second century when Pope Victor claimed that he had the right to decide the day on which everyone was to keep Easter. There was trouble in the third century, which provides our first evidence of appeal to the Petrine text of Matthew 16. There is a German monograph by Ludwig about the way that text was used by the ancient church. Also, Charles Pietri has recently written nearly 2000 pages on *Roma Christiana*, a history of the Roman community in the fourth and the first half of the fifth centuries. He argues in broad terms that the conversion of the great aristocratic families of Rome made possible the filling of Rome with noble churches, splendid mosaic and marble, and magnificent public processions, and that this helped to make possible the conquest of the old pagan city in time and space and thereby laid the foundations for Pope Leo the Great and his *plenitudo potestatis*.

P. Brown: It is a little more differentiated than that, with a great sense of nuance.

Shepherd: No one in the ancient church denied that those who held the see of Rome were successors of Peter; and the Roman see was always ranked first. But the effects of this varied in each individual situation in which the see of Rome intervened or was appealed to. In the case of Pope Victor, I agree with Professor LaPiana that it was an internal Roman dispute, trying to force the parish churches of Rome to agree with the bishop's date of Easter. Then the Asian church in Rome appealed to their confreres in Asia Minor, and that started the row on a larger scale. Certainly the case of Cyprian and Stephen is our first evidence for an appeal to the Petrine text in Matthew. In the fourth century, the Eastern bishops are prepared to use the Roman see when it would agree with them, and ignore it or oppose it otherwise. The situation involves a great many sociological and political factors that developed in the West. Certainly, Leo I was the first to give theoretical expression to the papal primacy, and also to attempt to exercise it, both doctrinally and jurisdictionally.

Wuellner: Professor Grant's Response showed that the idea of consensus was very much a calculated political move.

Shepherd: When he used the phrase *episcopus episcoporum*, Cyprian was really talking about himself, not the Bishop of Rome.

J. Wright: On p. 29, Professor MacMullen gives an interpretation of the grounding of the bishop's authority in his spirituality as ascetic and holy man, as meaning the power to make one's child die, or to make one sick. Is this really the bishop's spirituality, that it led to fear that he would "get you" if you did not obey?

Wuellner: And, according to Professor MacMullen, that is the one aspect distinctive about the bishop's authority.

Hobbs: I would be sorry if, in relation to the question of the primacy of Rome in the early centuries, we were to forget the landmark work already alluded to, Walter Bauer's *Rechtgläubigkeit und Ketzerei im ältesten Christentum*. It shows in great detail relative to certain parts of Eastern Christianity the great variety of means by which Rome attempted to establish at least theological and probably jurisdictional authority. His position was that intense pluralism existed in the early church, and history was rewritten backwards later to suggest a continuity of orthodoxy as represented by the church in Rome.

Caspary: The bishop lacks the *gladius* of the civil magistrate. He can excommunicate, but one can always then join the Donatists or become a pagan again. So if the bishop wants to protect his authority, he has recourse to spiritual means, the *gladius spiritualis*.

Gold: First, there is a kind of assumption that in 325 everything became immediately Christian. What happened to those who were not Christians then? Second, in this period there was a massive shift in the authority structure. Many factors were involved, and in many of them the Christian church played a significant role. Besides the theological factors, some highly significant political factors were alluded to in the paper and discussion. I use the Old Testament method of always asking the political question first. We should continue to lean toward the so-called "secular" questions.

P. Brown: The bishop as the patron of the poor and the undefended has to curse. The council of Macon in the 6th century says "We curse; for we have no other authority."* Any group with a notion of social justice has to have

---

*S.v. "Fluch," *Reallexikon für Antike und Christentum*.

its historiography which links misfortune to the disapprobation of those who stand for justice: this is what the curse is--a linking of misfortune with declared punishment for sin.

Do we ever have, in the classical world, the idea that one man can incorporate and sum up a community? It seems to make sense to a medieval and modern man, but not in the classical tradition.

Wuellner: Not even the philosopher?†

P. Brown: There is a difference between the latent role of a scholar or philosopher as the representative and the "core" of a value-system, and the bishop who is talked about as if he were able to sum up a community in his person.

Hobbs: Would the emperor be an exception?

Dillon: He is certainly the only candidate. A philosopher might be so regarded only in his own little group. He would never even seek such a hold over the people at large; he would despise it.

P. Brown: We are in danger of reading medieval views into the office of emperor. Office does not necessarily personify the community in the ancient world. That seems to me to be a breakthrough in the role of the bishop.

Buckley: To return to my previous question: I do not see any analog to the ferocity of orthodoxy (alluded to on p. 10) in the Sophists, or anywhere else, and the way the Christians were tearing each other's eyes out was a scandal to the pagans. Professor Shepherd's remarks on the consequences of making theologians bishops in the East were illuminating, but where are the roots of this kind of internecine conflict?

Chadwick: My view on p. 10 is attested in many ancient texts; I regret now that I did not overwhelm you with citations. The question at issue was, is heaven propitious, and how can it be maintained as friendly? That was the issue for Ambrose, and probably for the emperor.

Kolenkow: It is a commonplace that Roman secular law was quite harsh, and the bishop's court was mild. Bishops seemed to have encouraged secular action against heretics. Is there evidence that the secular powers handed people over to the bishop to mitigate the severity of the punishment?

Chadwick: In the ancient period, there was no case of the church handing anybody over to the secular arm, but there were many cases of the reverse. At one point, Leo the Great said that he was not sorry that the Priscillian-

---

†On the philosopher as one of the few outstanding individuals in Late Antiquity who summed up in his person the core of a cultural and religious tradition, see the position paper and responses in the *Protocol of the Thirty-Fourth Colloquy of the Center for Hermeneutical Studies* of Dec. 3, 1978 with Peter Brown on "The Philosopher and Society in Late Antiquity".

ists had been so roughly treated by Maximus. But Priscillian was not handed over to the secular arm by the church; he himself appealed to the secular arm against the church--and then no doubt regretted it.

J. Wright: I would not want to rule out the power of cursing, but surely spiritual authority is richer than that. Paul exercises spiritual authority writing to his churches, and from time to time there are intimations of cursing. But that hardly sums up Paul's spiritual authority.

The Old Testament gives us some views of an individual summing up a community, for example, the whole people being called Israel. If the bishop represents Christ, and Christ sums up the body of Christians, the roots of the summation may be Biblical, not Roman.

Hobbs: Paul used all sorts of means to establish his authority, but he usually tried moral suasion, plus his personal appearance in Corinth on one occasion--which was a total failure. Yet when his back was to the wall relative to the Galatians, he wrote nothing of his usual praise or thanksgiving, but did write "If anyone preaches a different gospel, even if it is an angel from heaven, let him be anathema." So Paul does not primarily engage in cursing, but he does provide a model and a precedent for the use of the curse as a last-ditch resort by the later episcopacy.

Dillon: As a footnote to the comment on p. 8 that "episcopal elections were normally a source of unrest and disorder. . . . The council of Serdica records its outrage at the practice of bribing a claque of laity to shout for a particular candidate." I have an example from the third century. In 238 Bishop Pontianus of Rome died, and was succeeded by Anteros, who died after a month--rather like recent events--and there was another election. Someone nobody expected, Fabian, was elected--he could well have been a Pole--because a dove flew into the chamber and landed on his head. Would you say this was a genuine miracle, or did Fabian's friends have a pet dove?

Chadwick: It is an enchantingly funny incident. (It also happened to Innocent X in 1644, although that dove actually settled on his cardinal's seat in the conclave.) Clearly, the church was divided and needed to settle it somehow; it could be called a singular providence that what could have been a bitter conflict was rapidly brought to such a happy conclusion by the introduction of this dove.

Dillon: There are, of course, two other possibilities. One, that it never happened at all, and the other that it was a fortuitous event. It is an unworthy thought, but it could have been quite a sophisticated political ploy.

Martin: There seem to be two types of anathemas, the one with effects that can be dramatically visible in this world, as happened to Ananias and Sapphira in Acts, and the "let them be anathema" type in the sense of "leave them to heaven." Which sort was it in the canon Professor Brown referred to?

Brown: It is an extremely short sentence, but I am not sure it is otherworldly. In the Muslim villages of northern Labanon, an anthropologist once asked why there were no miracles of cursing nowadays. The answer was, "There are no more landlords." Some people need cursing. A curse depends on a sense of justice, and on a training of a group's expectations of the ideal consequences of injustice. Misfortunes happen to many people, but at least we know why some of them happen to some people. Professor MacMullen was absolutely right in his emphasis; cursing is an extension of the bishop's arbitration.

Shepherd: We may call it superstition, but the early Christians looked for divine signs in the "fortuitous"--for example, in the election of Ambrose, who was not even baptized. I have been to a few episcopal elections, and no such extraordinary things have happened. But it is possible that such an assembly could have a certain sensitivity and perhaps overwroughtness, and something unexpected could lead them to make a choice they had not thought about to begin with.

Cyprian has some hair-raising examples of cursing.

Chadwick: On the subject of doves: Fabian was a surprising choice, but he did turn out to be a good bishop, and I see no reason why divine providence should confine itself to those acts in which human intention is involved.

I did not complain about Professor MacMullen's curses. It was probably most unusual for a bishop to curse out of personal pique. But apart from that, his last paragraph is historically accurate; it is what the ancient texts say. But to imply that the bishop's authority rested solely on fear would entail a massive value judgement about the nature and function of religion *in toto*. Of course there were elements of fear in early Christianity, as in modern Christianity. I would wish to interpret the remarks in a much wider setting.

I think the ancient church really did care for the poor, and also for women. There is good evidence for both. There is also good evidence that women liked the authority structure in the church the way it was--and perhaps still do. It must not be assumed that the Western world is necessarily normative for everywhere else.

The bishop's extraordinary position was not really quite as lonely as we sometimes picture it. It is important, for example, to recognize that when the bishop had his court, he had to have his presbyters sitting beside him on the bench. By canon law, he was not allowed to act alone.